Trueman Pickett

New Thought Preacher

Anita Trueman (Pickett) with the Peace Flag

Anita Trueman Pickett

New Thought Preacher

Lyn Burnstine

Skinner House Books
Boston

Published by Skinner House Books, an imprint of the Unitarian
Universalist Association, 25 Beacon Street, Boston, MA 02108-2800.

Printed in Canada.

Photos courtesy of John H. Pickett and Debby Merritt (frontispiece).

ISBN 1-55896-384-7

Library of Congress Cataloging-in-Publication Data
Burnstine, Lyn, 1933–
    Anita Trueman Pickett : New Thought preacher / Lyn Burnstine.
       p. cm.
    Includes bibliographical references.
    ISBN 1-55896-384-7 (pbk. : alk. paper)
    1. Pickett, Anita Trueman, 1881–1960.   2. Unitarian churches—
United States—Clergy—Biography.   3. New Thought.   I. Title.
BX9869.P52B87   1999
289.1'092—dc21
[B]   99-38657
                                          CIP

10 9 8 7 6 5 4 3 2 1
03 02 01 00 99

My thanks for support and encouragement go to members of Anita's family: her late daughters, Estelle Coggins and Laurel Stackpole; her grandchildren and their spouses, the late Anita Dougan, Ed Dougan, Carol Powell, Debbie and Sol Merritt, and John and Judy Pickett, who fed, nurtured, and cheered me on during my research. I am also grateful to my minister, the Reverend Dr. Linda Anderson, for her invaluable help; to Joan Goodwin for her generous spirit; to Skinner House for their vision in being willing to work with this first-time writer, and to the Unitarian Universalist Women's Federation for the 1994 Feminist Theology Award in the form of a grant to research and finish writing this book. My family and many friends also deserve thanks for their feedback, frequent proofreading, and tolerance for my obsession with Anita all these years.

Contents

Please see http://www.uua.org/bookstore/history/6130.html for a dramatic script of Anita Trueman Pickett's story, suitable for use in a worship service.

Introduction

Miss Anita Trueman is probably one of the most remarkable young women in the country.
                    —*Baltimore Sunday Herald* (circa 1900)

Possibly the most characteristic feature of the discourse was her admirable poise. Paderewski's principal power over his audiences is in his immediate assumption that he dominates it, and this may be said to be precisely the case with Miss Trueman.
                    —*The Washington Post*

Only eighteen years old, heir to philosophy of all ages. Besides being a philosopher, Miss Trueman is a poet. . . . She has made a sensation before Theosophical societies, labor conventions, teachers' associations and orthodox religious meetings. Even college professors have pronounced her utterances remarkable for so young a person.
                    —*The New York World*

She is pretty, with roguish looks, said to be Plato's reincarnation; lectures off-hand on any subject. Her audiences are in touch with her soul.
                    —*The New York Herald*

Miss Trueman is only a girl, and yet gray-haired men and women sit spell-bound, while in words always clear and earnest and sometimes impassioned, this girl teaches them their duty to themselves and to their fellowmen.
                    —*The Philadelphia North American*[1]

1

These newspaper quotes from around the turn of the century reflect the world's view of the young Anita Trueman. They were later printed in the mature Anita Trueman Pickett's promotional brochures for her lectures (so we are missing specific dates). As Anita Trueman Pickett neared the end of her life in the 1950s, she wrote an unpublished autobiography for her grandchildren. On page 1, she said:

> *I used to think, when you were growing up, that the world beyond the wharves and beaches of your island [Nantucket] was not more foreign to you than that of my childhood and youth. Even my children, now grandparents themselves, know very little of my life before I became their mother. Seldom, indeed, do the buried memories of those days come up to the surface of my consciousness. When, on Easter Day in 1908, I married your grandfather, I closed the book of a strangely adventurous youth, and only the advent of great-grandchildren has moved me to look over its pages again.*
>
> *For their sake and yours, I must tell the tale. It would seem like trying to recover memories of a former incarnation, were it not for the scrap-books of newspaper clippings, the bulging file of letters . . . the pile of printed programs and the stack of journals, which record the brief career of "the girl philosopher." These were buried in a trunk for years, carried from parish to parish and threatened at every move with destruction.*
>
> *Once when such a move was impending, I did reduce the bulk of this material by feeding some nineteen volumes of my diaries to the flames. As I sat by the blazing hearth, I lived again the spiritual struggles of my youth, the age-old tension between demands of a high calling and the hunger for home and parenthood.*

That theme consumed Anita's life: the ongoing struggle between calling and *kinder,* between career and *kuchen,* the two realities of her life. Although she was a woman far ahead of her time in many ways, she was also a product of her times, and suffered the conflicts engendered by her unusual upbringing and society's attitudes toward women—a source of constant frustration to her, yet always a vital force in shaping her decisions.

An ardent feminist, she wrote in her twenties of her resistance to the idea of marriage, calling it unnecessary and "a curse" to women (she even considered deliberate single motherhood), yet she so yearned for love and a family that she embraced the offer of both from her fellow student at Meadville Theological Seminary, Harold Lionel Pickett. She had resisted longer than many women of that time, marrying at 27, and she did so with the knowledge that marriage and motherhood might be so all-encompassing as to interfere with her preaching, lecturing, and writing career. Indeed, her life-long struggles persisted between the great demands put on her time and energy by her much-loved family and her need to fulfill the role for which she felt she was put on this earth—that of spiritual leader.

Anita's diaries abound with her cries of frustration at lack of recognition as her life progressed, yet her files at Harvard Divinity School Library, at Rowe Camp, and in her grandchildren's possession are voluminous. (Throughout this book, passages in Anita's own voice are italicized.) They speak of a full, rich life, unusual perhaps even for these times and *certainly* for a time when women's lives were still constricted almost as much as they were in the late 1800s—a time when, according to Cynthia Grant Tucker in *Prophetic Sisterhood,* "women . . . ended up in almost total obscurity, their presence expunged from the record by a conspiracy of forgetfulness." It is my mission to correct that obscurity.

I knew Anita during her last years. By then she was a woman in fragile health, modest, a bit cantankerous, feisty. I regret that I didn't take the time to hear her amazing stories from her own lips. I have paid a long (but joyful) penance for my youthful cavalier attitude toward the elderly by writing about her, in small increments, for nearly fifteen years. I have two motives. The first is to end the historical neglect of Anita Trueman Pickett's amazing life and her valuable contribution to women's role in the Unitarian Universalist ministry (the only mention of her in any previously published work is a small biography in Catherine F. Hitchings's book, *Unitarian and Universalist Women Ministers*). The second motive comes from Anita herself. Carolyn Heilbrun, in *Writing a Woman's Life,* says, "Biographers have sometimes written . . . of the palpable existence of their subjects." I *know* Anita wants me to write this book.

Anita's First Years
and the Paternal Influence

Anita Trueman was born in 1881 to Fanny and Willie Trueman, who had met in their native Birmingham, England, at the meetings of the Plymouth Brethren. Fanny was eight years Willie's senior. They were excited over the talk of the opportunities for free land in the backwoods of Canada, so after they had been married a year, they sailed for the new world on the cattleship *Brooklyn* and landed at Quebec in 1879. Fanny was pregnant with her first child—a girl, Lottie, who was to die from cholera shortly after her birth in 1880, following their move from Toronto to Cleveland in search of better work for Willie. The following April, Fanny's arms were filled with another child. "Square Baby" or "Annie" were the names used for this chubby, healthy little girl, who would choose her own name—Anita, the Spanish version of Annie—many years later when she first began to publish her writings.

Willie was a furniture maker, and Anita's unpublished autobiography told of how he had made a neat polished box for their savings with a slit in the top and a flap of felt under it, which effectively prevented the premature removal of the contents. The bottom was screwed on securely, only to be unscrewed to pay for this new baby, but then they would start saving for their dearest dream, a return to England. Ten months later when they opened the box, it contained just enough to pay for their passage to England on a cattleship. "That box is one of my treasures now," Anita wrote in her seventies. Another souvenir of that period, which her father helped to build, was a black velvet and gilt shield, one of many which were used to fasten the draperies of the catafalque that carried President Garfield through the streets of Cleveland to his last resting place.

While living back in Birmingham, England, near their families, Fanny gave birth to two more children. Ernest lived for only seven months, then Gertrude was born, "a tiny thing weighing less than four pounds with a congenital spinal curvature. The doctor had no hope of her survival, but mother put all her willpower to work with single-minded devotion, and saved her baby," maintained Anita. The five-year-old Anita was sent to live with her grandparents, seeing her parents only on weekends.

The Plymouth Brethren, the Quakers with whom Anita began her spiritual life, were a dour lot "with an overwhelming preoccupation of salvation and a very real conflict with a personal devil day by day," she reported, adding that she knew she was very wicked, yet sure that she was saved. She loved to testify in the meetings of the Plymouth Brethren and was very worried about the state of salvation of her beloved grandfather Trueman, who all agreed was not saved. "I used to labor with him about his soul, sometimes sitting on his knee," Anita wrote. She never learned what his sins were until years later, when her father told her about his life as a boy in the tavern on the Essex Road, in stagecoach days. Then the master of the house—her grandfather—would sometimes imbibe too freely of the wicked liquids which were kept on tap for customers. His energetic wife would be compelled to take over the management of the inn, and on more than one occasion dragged Willie, her youngest, with her into her bedroom, to pray tearfully for her malingering husband.

The children ate beef drippings instead of butter and were not allowed to speak at table unless an adult addressed them. They ate rice pudding because "it was good for us and because the queen approved of it." If Anita sulked over the strong, tough cabbage, she was punished. If she talked back, she had to stand in a corner with her back to the room, saying over and over again to the devil, "Come down, Proud Spirit." "This perpetual struggle with the devil and the practice of hounding one another about their sins seems to have been characteristic of the Birmingham Plymouth Brethren," Anita wrote.

[T]his [public confession] did not seem necessary to Grandpa. He was at peace with himself, and confounded

them all by dying as calmly as he had lived. My mother's people were Plymouth Brethren, too . . . but they were not belligerent about it.

In Anita's later years, she was to comment on her experiences with Quakers: "I have always been charmed by the combination of austerity and spiritual pride which they embody." She went to a meeting with friends, and their mother said to her, "If the Spirit moves thee, speak." During a long, weighty silence, Friends sitting on both sides of her nudged her, at which she thought, "Verily the Spirit hath elbows!"

During the early years of Anita's life, her father had built up a good woodworking business. When he sold it and went to work for the Lancaster Company, makers of fine photographic apparatus, he entered a field that would occupy him for the rest of his work life. For a time, Willie Trueman was being sent back and forth to America by the Lancaster Company, so Fanny—always nervously concerned about finances—took advantage of his absence to establish an English-style boarding house. There were a part-time gardener and handyman, two maids, and a governess. The servants and Anita slept in the attic of the house, whose windows opened on a parapet surrounding all four mansions—theirs was one of a block of four. "It was my great joy to steal out there after being put to bed, to feel so near to the sky, and to God, for I was still earnestly religious," she wrote.

In his travels between England and America, Willie had begun to espouse the theories of Col. Robert Ingersoll, the noted agnostic lawyer-lecturer. He had discarded the theology of the Plymouth Quakers and escaped from their discipline. His brown eyes sparkled with enthusiasm as he talked of his newfound libertarianism. Small wonder that he found little response and some violent rejection among his own family. Fanny was horrified at his ideas and anxious lest he should offend the tenants. Only the governess seemed to understand him. The Plymouth meeting formally disowned Willie and the governess was sent packing!

In 1891 Willie returned to America and employment with the Anthony Company—a firm comparable to the Lancaster Company in England. Accepting a position as their branch manager in Greenpoint, Brooklyn, he persuaded the family to rejoin him in

America and establish a new home. The ten-year-old Anita's joy at returning to "my native land" was short-lived when she encountered teasing and rudeness at the hands of her schoolmates. This was during a time when Americans were "twisting the lion's tail," a bad time for a sensitive, over-weight child with bunchy clothes and a British accent to be introduced to the American public school.

Anita was ahead of her age in reading, but her arithmetic was all wrong, being pegged to English money. This led to a humiliating experience of being put in a lower grade to learn American terms and measures. The teacher who helped Anita adjust to American life, Lida Murphy, attended one of her lectures a few years later; she said that she had expected some unusual development from such an odd child. They laughed together over Anita's habit of doing her paperwork as swiftly as possible in order to lay her head down on the desk and think. "Such mooning was not permitted at home," Anita wrote.

Willie Trueman was always a profound influence on his daughter, and, as he pursued the teaching and ideas of his mentor, Colonel Ingersoll, Anita began to be convinced by the oratory and the printed lectures, which she considered "a challenge to the thinker." She and her mother were "setting up a battle of prayer for his soul," still attending a meeting of the Brethren while also attending a Methodist Mission Sunday school, where Anita enjoyed the organ music and stained glass windows condemned by the Brethren as worldly. Her teacher took Anita's salvation very seriously, knowing about William Trueman's agnosticism, and knowing that Anita herself had been reading Ingersoll. She took Anita with her to teachers' prayer meetings, where the entire staff prayed for the young girl's salvation. "It was an awesome feeling," Anita wrote, "having your name spoken before God in this way," and it started her on a soul-searching period that was also mind-stretching. Between the prayer meetings and long arguments with her father, she sought "in passionate meditation" the answer to her soul's need.

Anita and her father found common ground in reading Ralph Waldo Emerson's essays; she made a ceremony of going to her Methodist church school teacher to announce that she was really a Transcendentalist and could never join the Methodist Church. In taking this stand, she was really making sacrifices, since she adored the teacher and was grieved to see her no more. Anita loved the hearty singing of gospel hymns and missed the occasional celebrations, particularly the annual Sunday school parade, a Brooklyn institution.

Also in taking this stand, she separated herself forever from mainstream religions. From that day forward, she explored other denominations, but always came back to Free Thought[2] beliefs, forming her opinion of God and spiritual life on the basis of reason rather than on dogma or doctrine, independent of authority.

When she graduated as valedictorian from Brooklyn Grammar School in 1896, her family had already moved to New Haven, leaving her behind with friends, whose small children she cared for in exchange for room and board. "The Responsibility of the Rising Generation" was the subject of her valedictory, about which she wrote in her seventies, saying that there was nothing original or promising about it—yet she recalled that delivering it was one of the thrills of her life. Little did she dream then that it was to be the first of several thousand such appearances. "My generation did not fulfill my dream, but I certainly did mine," was her observation.

In New Haven, her father's job became so frustrating that it made him ill. Fanny encouraged him to resign, and the family returned to Brooklyn, where once again Willie set up a woodworking shop and did repair jobs for the Anthony Company. Anita wrote that in this enterprise she spent happy days as her father's partner. For the first time, she realized how much he had always wished she were a boy: "I had to prove that I could work as well as a boy." She tried to fill the bill as a worker as well as in sharing his intellectual life. They made thousands of advertising novelties—some of them designed by Anita. She made the working drawings for the patent on his invention of a nonwarping roller for carrying the backgrounds used in photographic studios; the Anthony Company ordered a large number of these.

Anita mixed the glue, kept the books, did the sweeping, and prepared lunch. When, in time, there were more orders to fill, she worked on the lathe and at the finishing bench varnishing delicate woodwork, as well as japanning and gilding iron work. They had bought a job lot of machines in a junk yard, and cleaning them up and finding ways to use them were of great satisfaction to Anita, who confessed that she had a feeling for tools and machinery; she wondered whether that period of working with her father engendered it or whether it was in her blood before she was born. "I love the scream of the saw and the hum of the planer, and the smell of steaming wood as the heat of friction releases forest fragrances. Factories of all kinds fascinate me, but a wood-working shop wins my heart," she said.

An ongoing motif in Anita's life—a love for woodworking, a love for building and making things—grew from these experiences wherein her home was always a workshop. Whatever work her father was doing was shared by her mother. One of Anita's earliest memories was of helping to put the upholstery tacks in chairs that he was seating.

During her long ride to work, she read the Ingersoll, Emerson, Thomas Carlyle, and Edward Bellamy works that she would later discuss with her father en route home—a home where it was not yet possible to talk of these things. Her mother insisted on taking her place in the shop and sending her to high school in the fall of 1896, a move intended to prevent her from becoming too masculine and to give her the advantage of further education.

Her father's response to the suggestion that she belonged in the College Preparatory Course rather than the Commercial Course was that he "knew as much about college as a cow does about Sunday." His scorn for conventional education derived from his own child-hood in England where there were no free schools. With less than a year of school, but possessing an eager mind, he had taught himself how to learn—"how to *know,*" as Anita explained. "He had an uncanny ability in practical mathematics. He could figure out the cost of such a complicated article as a camera in a few minutes, whereas his highly educated office staff would take a couple of days and many pages of calculations to reach the same result."

Anita's father was a life-long reformer. Hardly a day went by without his "supplying the newspapers with mental pablum," as Anita commented, and hundreds of those letters were preserved in his copybook. She observed that they were exceptionally clear and sensible, and those cast in the form of parables were delightfully amusing, "though their humor must have undercut some substantial citizens' pomposity."

Returning to manage the Anthony Company in New Haven in 1898, Willie was active in local politics as well as Single Tax activities—Henry George's concept of a single tax based on unimproved land values. During his term as alderman-at-large, someone who "knew the inside of his mind," according to Anita, wrote the following in a newspaper article:

> William Trueman naturally is a man who will be much misunderstood, because he wants people to do things they have never done before, and for their own benefit. There always have been such men and they usually have been well scolded, and a few years back occasionally burned, hanged, broken on the wheel, or delicately quartered, and nailed up in fragments on city walls. Mr. Trueman's chief offense consists in his belief that present systems of taxation are inequitable, that they tax the poor man more than they do the rich man, that they enable some to live without working, and prevent others from living though they work. A great many other people possibly have the same feeling stowed away in the recesses of their minds, but are not thoughtless enough to jar a complacent world by talking too loudly about it.
>
> The world is a slow old poke and the man who tries to make her walk faster than she intends to must expect the rough side of her tongue sometimes. Those who know Mr. Trueman know, however, that he consoles himself with the thought that his doctrine will prevail in his children's time, if not in his. And besides, he has been elected an alderman-at-large, which proves that the people of New Haven admire his pluck, if they do not always take his medicine. He probably will make a record for faithful service and wise effort, and the city will be benefitted by his presence on the Board.

Anita acknowledged that her father lasted only one term as an alderman but, besides winning vigorous enemies, he was instrumental in getting the tax commission to make a new appraisal of real estate, in which land values and improvements were listed separately. She asserted that the result was a clear demonstration of Henry George's Single Tax contention that the assessment of land values was practically automatic, while discovering the value of improvements required a large number of full-time experts, and was

11

even then only approximate. When Willie Trueman accepted a job with Eastman Kodak in 1905, he had a twinge of conscience about offering himself to "the trust," and his fears were justified when the New Haven papers gloated in huge headlines, "TRUST GETS WILLIAM TRUEMAN."

In anticipation of the move to Rochester, New York, to manage Eastman Kodak's Century Company factory, Willie sold the New Haven house and purchased a farm in Kingston, New York, together with his brother-in-law, Edward Harris from England, who was to manage it. This arrangement soon proved untenable and Fanny took over the management of the farm for nine months of the year, spending only the winter months with her husband in Rochester. The Panoram and Graflex cameras were developed under Willie's supervision, but later, when large cameras were made obsolete by the invention of modern photographic equipment, the Century Camera Works was closed and he was dismissed. So, in 1910, Willie came back to Kingston to live full-time at the farm. Anita reported that although he made a valiant but never successful effort to farm, he remained there until his death in 1926.

Anita was proud of her father, of his having been elected an alderman in New Haven and of his service on the school board and board of elections while living out his final years in Kingston, New York. He earned a citation for selling Liberty Bonds during World War I, and presented himself as a candidate for the State Assembly. As Anita observed, "As a Democrat, his defeat was assured in this solidly Republican district, but the campaign gave him one more opportunity to indulge his gift of oratory."

In Anita's early diaries and the segments of her autobiography taken from those diaries, she wrote almost exclusively of her father's positive influence on her and his encouragement of her endeavors. A letter she wrote to her Uncle Harry in England in 1899 survives in her father's old copybook and demonstrates how much she identified with her father and his philosophy. In it Anita responds to a criticism of her former letter to her uncle. It says, "Of what shall I write, if not of my philosophy? Our home life owes its many joys hereto. My own life, like my father's is utterly bound up in a continuous endeavor to serve and uplift humanity."

There are, however, small clues to be found to William Trueman's negativism and lack of support in a few passages, such as one wherein she deplores his commending her for her housekeeping but "persistently ridiculing my poetic effusions." Another one occurred in 1904 when, having ended a formal engagement, she was told that if she did not marry she must become economically useful. Both she and her sister Gertrude, who by then had secured a diploma from Yale Business College, were being strongly encouraged by their parents to be self-supporting. Her father did not consider Anita's preaching and lecturing, by then bringing her much fame but little remuneration, to constitute a legitimate career.[3] Anita wrote that she and Gertrude both felt that to do so was impossible in New Haven, where they were known as William Trueman's daughters, associated with his "unpredictable agitations." Although Anita obviously worshipped her father, it was clear that he was an opinionated, stubborn, and difficult man.

In diary passages from Anita's mature years, she often agonized over her parents' relationship problems: they often lived rather separate lives for periods of time and, in 1906, even considered a total separation. A telling passage in Anita's writings tells of her father's behavior during the Truemans' silver wedding anniversary, when he made a speech that "amazed and chagrined me. Not a word about Mother, who had carried major burdens of those twenty-five years with him! But with glee and his inimitable sarcasm, he traced the course of his own life, and his recent successes, as if he had done it all alone." Anita's most honest appraisal of the balance between the admirable and the not-so-admirable qualities of William Trueman are to be found in this passage that she penned after his death in 1926:

There was no organic trouble—just the accumulated worry and weariness of an unbalanced life. Never would he consent to enjoy himself. Always it annoyed him to see other people having a good time. His theories of life dominated and enslaved him, so that he could not adjust himself to life as it is. The martyr complex was strong in him, and he never could believe that people cared for him. He wanted to drive them into a bare Utopia that did not attract them, and his method was a harsh one, for he had a perfect genius for invective. The strange thing is that this power of sarcasm, which he used so freely and in which he took such pride, is the thing which people forgave because he had so many other good qualities.

I think very often of my father, but somehow do not feel him near me. Is he resting after the wearisome journey of life, or has he found some paradise of reformers where per-petual argument insulates the soul from reality? . . . [T]he time will come again when we shall be together and he will help me with my earthly task (or some task of other spheres).

A Public Speaking
Career Begins

The story of William Trueman's influence on Anita and her eventual life pursuits would be incomplete without the chronicle of their mutual involvement with the Single Tax movement of writer, philosopher, and economist Henry George. She declared that "this was the experience which determined the trend of my life." After a brief foray into "Bellamy-style Socialism," which she and her father found lacking in single-mindedness and agreement among its proponents, they became ardent Single Taxers. George's *Progress and Poverty* delighted them with its "clarity and completeness."[1]

In George's 1897 campaign as the Jeffersonian Democrats' candidate for the mayoralty of Greater New York, the Greenpoint sector headquarters were in William Trueman's shop. Although William was not yet a citizen, and Anita was a woman and so could not vote, they enthusiastically swung into the campaign. They knew their candidate could not win, but saw the campaign as a valuable forum for political education. Anita told of how they rejoiced in this chance to preach Henry George's gospel of "equal opportunity to all, full reward to craftsman or artist in the possession of the fruits of his effort, and ample support for community activities and improvements, through a *single tax* on land values."

Anita's father had not been supportive of her poetic efforts except that, she said, "If I harness my muse to the car of reform, he was willing that I should ride it." He now encouraged her to write a campaign poem, "The Advance of the People." In reciting it and giving impromptu talks at the street meetings, Anita felt "the joy of martyrdom when some women in the crowd called me a 'bold hussy.' I was wearing that fall a pretty red plush jacket, and a matching tam with three small ostrich plumes set upright, Prince o'Wales style, and I was pleased when it was audibly admired."

Anita's teachers were not happy with the campaign's effect on her grades—she had shown great promise as a freshman with the highest grades ever recorded in the Brooklyn Girls' High School—so they pleaded with her to "keep out of politics." Her response was to beg for patience for the duration of the campaign—that to her it was not politics, but reform, and therefore deserving of her loyalty. In her old age she maintained that, in retrospect, she believed that it was a better education for her than any school could have given.

Anita had already begun public speaking with an address at the Brooklyn College of Music and Metaphysics. That opportunity had come about when she was squelched by her own school's authorities from expounding on her views of education—her vision of her generation as destined to transform the world, and her belief that education ought to be preparing them for this high mission, that "it should invite the student to unfold his potentialities through training in the art of thinking," and not, as had been expressed to her by a teacher, that "education means acquiring knowledge, the accumulation of facts." Anita's lecture titled "The True Philosophy of Education" was presented at the invitation of W. J. Colville, an Englishman and a preacher of the gospel of spiritual freedom and fellowship who was destined to become a dear friend and supporter of Anita's writing and lecturing efforts. She had been introduced to his lectures, a dozen a week in three or four cities, through her family's attendance at the Church of Individual Dominion, Francis E. Mason's church. Mason had been an early associate of Mary Baker Eddy. Although he had too much individuality to submit to her domination, he recognized that her truth was universal and presented it in a dynamic fashion. It was the first time that Anita's entire family had been in agreement about worship since the days of the Plymouth Brethren.

As election day approached, Anita recited her poem at a mass meeting before the largest audience she had yet faced. She was scheduled to introduce the candidate, Henry George himself, at a meeting the very next night—four days before the coming election. She said, "How eagerly I anticipated the opportunity to publicly honor him in his presence." This was not to be, for Henry George suddenly collapsed and died that very day, October 29, 1897. His doctors had warned him that the strain of the campaign might be more than he could endure, but, according to Anita, his decision was that "there could be no better way to die than in giving his last strength for the education of the people in the principles and techniques of equal opportunity."

At the meeting that night, with Henry George, Jr.'s name substituted for his father's on the ballot, several of the leaders tried and failed, in their overwhelming sorrow, to address the crowd:

> *Then a great power seemed to rise within me, and I took the floor. "This is what Henry George would say to you if he could speak," I began, and went on passionately to urge them to carry on the work. It was just what the others had been trying to say, but they were older and more weary. My eager dedication of my own youth seemed to hearten them. When I sat down, one of them took from a bookshelf a copy of* Progress and Poverty *and read the closing pages, one of the greatest sermons ever penned. We went home with Henry George's own words ringing in our hearts, words that were to be cast in bronze on the monument erected by the citizens and schoolchildren of Greater New York, "He who will hear, to him the clarions of the battle call. How they call, and call, and call, 'til the heart swells that hears them! Strong soul and high endeavor, the world needs them now!"*

Anita was part of the huge throng of citizens who filed past George's body as it lay in state at the Grand Central Palace. When Edward McGlynn, the radical priest who had dared excommunication to support the cause, began his oration with the words, "There was a man sent of God, and his name was Henry George," the electric hush of attention broke into a spontaneous cheer. "The great soul departed from that frail body among the flowers had entered into the hearts of the multitude," Anita wrote.

The experience of Henry George's death had left Anita with a sense of mission, eager to give a message to the world of his doctrine of "equal opportunities for all; special privileges for none." She believed that complicated problems of social and economic distress untangled themselves so easily when the simple Single Tax principle—that of taxing land according to its base value and not its improvements—was applied to them, just as some proven formula in algebra could be used to solve difficult mathematical propositions. The reasoning in this delighted her and she proclaimed, "I was madly eager to tell others about it." She would espouse George's theories, speak to Single Tax organizations, and preach his message from the pulpit of many churches throughout her lifetime. The poem she wrote for his campaign, "The Advance of the People" (which can be found in the Readings section at the end of this book) was soon followed by a memorial poem, "The Martyr, Henry George."

In Anita's collection of memoirs is a handwritten note from Henry George, Jr., that reads:

> Go on in your work my young friend, but remember those who work for the public good are looked upon as enemies to the public. I have found the continuity of life a fact and shall certainly work for the overthrow of ignorance which has been fostered by the churches.

Going back to the mundane world of schoolwork and housekeeping was hard for Anita after this great experience. While laboring over geometry problems that had been neglected during the campaign, she often found herself drifting into a reverie in which she beheld herself addressing a crowd. She would stand in her little study, pouring forth torrents of oratory in a whisper, fearing lest the family might disturb her in her fantasy.

Later, as a young woman still living in her parents' home in New Haven, Connecticut, Anita would organize the New Haven Women's Single Tax Club. She would go as their delegate to a meeting of the National Women's Single Tax League in New York City in 1902 and speak at many of the league's meetings and conventions in subsequent years. In later life, she explained to her grandchildren, "If it seems strange to you that a Movement as slim in proportions as Single Tax should segregate the sexes in its work, you must remember that women were not yet citizens in the United States, so that their work was restricted to persuasion and education."

Because most of Anita's talks and sermons were never written down—her ability to speak with only notes became legend—there are no existing copies of her addresses on the Single Tax. However, in an article written around 1940, she responds to a review in the *Christian Register* regarding Single Tax. It is entitled "Grinding the Georgean Axe" and can be found in the Readings section at the end of this book.

Spiritual Journey

After a time of fervent concentration on the public good, Anita Trueman was delving into the meaning of individual existence. In meditation she was asking the question, "Who am I and what am I here for?" Frank Mason's vigorous preaching and Colville's extensive metaphysics had opened an inner world to her that made the Brooklyn Girls' High School and the Truemans' dingy flat seem "merely external incidentals." One day in 1897, while scrubbing the floors on hands and knees (her Saturday chore), she experienced a moment when the splashing of the water in the pail reminded her of a brook rippling over stones on a wooded hillside:

> *Instantly, that cosmic sense which I had been cultivating in my meditations responded to the picture. Yes, even this water that tumbles out of the faucet, even the dirty water I pour down the sink, is part of an endless fluid movement of all matter. Silver clouds in the summer sun are part of the circle. Lines of blank verse were dancing five-footed across my imagination as I went back to my scrubbing and finished the task in an exalted dream.*

The poem sang in her head all through that night of preparing supper, clearing up, Saturday night bathing, mending stockings, and blacking high-button shoes for Sunday morning wear. It woke her early, and she crept through her parents' room to the tiny hall room she called her study, where she wrote out, with scarcely a pause, a poem called "The Fall of Man," in which she formulated her theory of human existence.

This teenager was in love with words, and could never rest until a mood or inspiration had been clothed in imagery and translated into language. But even at this stage, it was the communion of the spoken word that drew her; audiences were already demanding recitations of her poems. Her youthful enthusiasm and her natural gift for speaking took the place of profound and complicated reasoning.

William Trueman printed "The Fall of Man" together with her poem about Henry George and three others in a booklet. Part of "The Fall of Man" was printed in a paper called *The Faith and Hope Messenger,* the organ of the Faith and Hope Association in Boston. Part of it was lost over the years, but a few of the verses remain, written by the teenage Anita after her epiphany over the scrub bucket. They can be found in the Readings section at the end of this book.

Anita stated that this application of modern metaphysics made the Eden fable vital to her and to her audiences and defined the sad state of mankind as a whole, while giving an immediate impetus to the desire for self-improvement. She added that most people needed only a few ringing words and an infusion of faith to awaken them from their lethargy, then continued:

> *The Light of Consciousness shining in such souls as Jesus and Gautama, has lifted multitudes to higher levels. But not until we ourselves grasp this torch can we begin to overcome the darkness and delusion of ignorance. The differences between people are in the depth and range of their consciousness.*

As Anita reflected on this philosophy from the vantage of her seventy-eighth year, she observed:

> *. . . I am well satisfied that it was a good philosophy to live and teach. It has made my whole life fascinating, and enhanced its precious moments. It has carried me through periods of tragedy, and it stands by me in these days when the physical organism is losing its resiliency. Having shared in the creative life of my universe, having drifted through periods of weakness and pain, I know the meaning of Life's*

*great rhythms, and flow with them toward the ultimate
unity.*

Anita asserted, in her last years, that the cosmic vision behind
the poem remained constant with her, and that all the religious and
spiritual movements she encountered seemed to serve that one
central truth—the philosophy she had formulated for herself at age
sixteen. She surely did not mean to imply that her truth had been
static and unchangeable, for she often affirmed that she found truth
in all teachings while embracing many forms of religion on her spiritual quest. Her confession of faith, written near the end of her life,
closes with these lines:

> *Every place I visit is holy ground.*
> *All persons I meet are Divine Companions,*
> *seeking me as I seek them,*
> *That we may reveal the Divine in our souls one to another,*
> *And share the Divine that we discover in our Universe.*

Many years hence, Unitarian Universalists would enthusiastically
embrace the concept of the interdependent web—not unlike the
young Anita's vision of "at-one-ness."

One of the spiritual paths that Anita followed for a time was
that of Spiritualism.[1] Her brief foray into that religion and her eventual connection with a Spiritualist church began in this way. Her
father had been struggling with a career decision when Mr. W. J.
Colville suggested he see the noted psychic Ira Moore Courlis. The
prophecy that Courlis gave him—that he would soon hear from
someone within the Anthony firm—came true in a matter of hours,
when Mr. Anthony sent for Willie to come back to New Haven and
take complete charge of the factory there.

Courlis was then conducting evening meetings in the same
Masonic temple where the Truemans attended Francis Mason's
morning sermons. After giving an impromptu "inspirational" talk,
he would conduct a period of "tests," during which a medium under
control gave messages to people in the audience from their departed friends and relatives. Anita's parents attended a few of these meetings before they moved to New Haven. Certain Spiritualists were
sure that with a little training Anita would be a remarkable medi-

um. In fact, there were remunerative openings for her at once, if she would only "give up her control." She fought this temptation, then and on later occasions. The Truemans' move to New Haven and a new residence helped to eliminate the danger. She reacted to these heady influences with what she called a "certain arrogance." She went on to say:

> Never *would I surrender my reason and my will to the control of another being. . . . I could see that such surrender would mean loss of individuality. The center of Divine Intelligence within me is supreme; the lesser grades of consciousness through which I relate myself to my environment, must be polarized to this center only. Between me and my companions, visible or not, there must be the interplay of equals. If there are master-souls, visible or not, who have resolved the problems of mortality, I seek them with reverence but not submission. They will not try to control me; they will hail and inspire me; they will delight in stimulating by their love and leadership, that inner consciousness in which I am one with the divine. . . . So renunciation was required.*

While all of this struggle was going on internally, Anita recalled, "I looked like a fat young female, trotting to school every day, and striving to catch up with neglected studies." Her tendency toward obesity continued into her teenage years and was a great trial to her. As late as 1900, a Providence reporter was to write that "her figure betokens corpulence in later life." The same writer said she had a "decidedly Roman nose," which led her to discount his prophecy. In her seventies, she wrote, "As a matter of fact, my corpulence was behind me then. I have been underweight ever since I was eighteen, when a long spell of malaria undermined my health, and left me with the chronic anemia from which I have always suffered."

Later in her preaching career, when she was 21, she was to speak often in Spiritualist churches in Baltimore, Maryland; Washington, D.C.; Alliance, Ohio; and Philadelphia, Pennsylvania, but always with the condition that there be no "tests" during her programs, determined as she was not to mix her work with mediumship. She answered the question that this surely raises for the reader when she wrote in her autobiography that, considering her initial hostility to certain phases of Spiritualism and a continuing critical attitude toward its materialism and sensationalism, she was amazed to find in her journals the written proof that she continued to work in that field. She offered the explanation that modern psychology had not yet put psychic phenomena in their place, and also that, in many respects, these were truly liberal churches offering a home for free-thinkers. She was adamant in her refusal to be classified by any label, and felt that she had something to share with all people. She would speak for any group that invited her, she said, and "I must admit that the Spiritualist Churches paid me well, and allowed me complete freedom of thought and expression."[2]

Once during this time, she found her parents indulging in a series of seances and entertaining a famous medium. She commented that it made her rather sick at heart, but that the medium was later found to be in possession of physical aids to "materialization" and "this brought the Spiritualist chapter in our [family's] history to a close." During this same time, around 1901, she spent some months intensely studying Catholicism, which held a great attraction for her. While still struggling with her decision whether to become Catholic—a time she referred to as her "Catholic Pilgrimage"—she wrote in her journal:

> *I am whatever I touch. I have been a Mental Scientist, a Theosophist, a Spiritualist, a Vedantist, a Bahaist. Yet I have never once changed my base or compromised my position. Now, I find myself a Catholic. I have found a new way of "tasting and adoring God." Yet I am not changed—I have simply added to my experience.*
>
> *I shall never be the slave of any cult. I shall never acknowledge any limitation. All institutions, to include me, must become universal, and none shall exclude me, for they are all mine. They shall serve me. I will have them purer, grander, better than they are. I will combat nothing. I will seek the soul of all. I will encourage and serve them all.*

Anita confided that she seemed to hear the sweet voice of the Eternal Mother, saying to her, "This, too, Child, is one of thy experiences. Here also hast thou found truth. Here have I held communion with thee. . . . Drink of this cup. Taste its joys. Feel its bondage. Know what it means to the multitudes who embrace it. But remember, little one, thou art mine, and mine alone. I must have thee free. I have prepared thy work and arranged the plan. . . . All churches, institutions, organizations, shall contribute to thee, that thou mayest in turn reveal the soul of them to the people. This is thy mission and my will." Anita added that she accepted the word of the voice that she calls "O Most Perfect Mother." She remarked that she had lent her voice to the support of many causes, and "step by step I have advanced toward the ideal of universal love, and as my love has expanded, my understanding has increased." Still, she agonized over the desire she felt for all that the Church seemed to offer, and prayed:

> *O, most Holy One, guard my heart and guide my feet. Let nothing win me away from Thy spirit of Universal Love and Compassion. . . . I would I might be a Catholic and yet retain the freedom and follow the work that claims me now. . . . But as a minister of truth, the sky is my temple and my Journal my confessor. How will it end, I wonder. How will these pages read, in years to come? You hold a strange record, little book.*

Anita wrote that the time might come when she would become a member and attendee of the Church, but that she did not believe that the Catholic Church "holds the keys of Heaven and guards the gates of Hell!" She continued, saying that she had no fear concerning the afterlife and did not believe that this life determined all eternity for all people—that "what we are here determines what we shall be forever." Further soul-searching brought her to a final decision about the Catholic Church, chronicled in her journal of 1902:

> *I cannot connect fear with religion, nor bow down before dogmas which seem unreasonable and cruel to me. I could enter the Church and derive many benefits from communion with it. But I could not set aside the Oriental teachings which are so dear to me, and the conception of the Universe which was revealed to me. . . . I cannot become less than I am. The Divine is Universal. It is not contained in any*

Church, though it may be revealed more directly through one than through others.

Anita believed that the Catholic Church could help her to live a holy life, but feared that it would cut her off from communion with truth in other forms. She wrote that she must be free for the work that awaited her, and if the Catholic Church proposed to set bounds to her genius, she could not embrace it. Her conviction was "born in my soul" that she must still remain independent of all institutions, as she had done in the past. She professed to her belief that "All religions are aids to the soul in its search after God. I hail them all!"

This great experience was over. It had been of immeasurable value to her, for it brought her, as she explained, "into communion with the souls of millions of my companions." It brought her knowledge of and sympathy with what she considered the greatest religious institution in the world; it gave her the key to the treasure house of art. She wrote, "Now I am no longer a stranger in the Catholic Church. I belong to the soul of the Church, but not to its body."

Literary Friendships

January 1898 found the Truemans back in New Haven, with Anita registering at a new high school under her newly chosen name—Anita, rather than Annie. It was a school with more boys than girls, dominated by secret societies in imitation of the Yale fraternities, leaving the awkward newcomer out in the cold. She didn't like the students; they found her pretensions to being a writer and her Brooklyn accent sources of amusement. The Trueman home, however, was becoming a center of philosophical and economic discussion, as they had organized a Single Tax Club—with William as president and Anita as secretary—that became a real power in New Haven. Later, the club entertained the Women's National Single Tax League; surviving photographs show the delegates and speakers grouped in front of the Truemans' Edgewood Avenue house.

During the next summer, Fanny Trueman went to England. While her mother was not there to protest, Anita had no trouble at all convincing her father, who scorned conventional education, to allow her to give up the pursuit. She had already begun holding discussion sessions following courses of lectures given by W. J. Colville at the Truemans' home, and had begun several series of talks on "The Evolution of Individuality." This led to speaking engagements in New Haven and surrounding towns, so she never returned to Hillhouse High School on Orange Street. Although Anita had not yet begun keeping a journal, her father's copy-press book survives to this day, and holds five hundred paper-thin vellum pages, mostly letters from both of them, that verify dates and events—an invaluable aid as she wrote her autobiography seventy years later: "My own letters of the period . . . reveal the strange child that I was, born grown up in certain ways, and destined never to grow up in others."

29

Many of these letters were written on behalf of the Single Tax Movement—to newspapers, to other reformers, and to well-known people of the day who were known to be in sympathy with the movement. Her first assignment, in March 1899, for the Single Tax Letter Writing Corps, was to write to the author of "The Man with the Hoe." Edwin Markham had become a national figure from this popular poem. Her letter in the copybook is barely decipherable, but she translated part of it for her autobiography. Out of four pages, she was able to recover these few lines:

> [T]he widespread publication and powerful influence of the poem have made you a national character so that I feel, as a loyal American woman and an active worker in the field of social reform, I may take the liberty of personally addressing you. I will state first that I am an advocate of the Single Tax, and it is my purpose in the present letter to ask your attention to it as a method of social reform advocated by thousands of men and women who like yourself have seen "the emptiness of ages" gazing through the hollow eyes of outraged humanity, so well typified by the figure in Millet's great picture.

The letter concludes thus:

> The Single Tax cause needs writers and poets, men and women of ardent purpose and earnest thought. You should be among their ranks. For want of a great poet, bloody wars have been fought, and ghastly rebellions have watered beautiful countries with blood. Ella Wheeler Wilcox, our Queen of Poesy here in the East stands hand in hand with us. There is work for you to do, and the time is ripe.

Anita mailed the letter to Oakland, California, feeling that she had done her duty, little knowing what "rich fruit this letter would bear in my life." She continued: "I do not remember that the S. T. Letter Writing Corps ever gave me another assignment, but I am everlastingly grateful to them for this one." From this introduction came a warm friendship that enriched her life for years to come.

Markham's answer, on May 6, 1899, indicated that he thought the letter to be from an older woman. It read, in part:

> It gave me great pleasure to receive your thoughtful and earnest letter of April 28th. Let me assure you that I am in full sympathy with your protest against our social injustice. I am in sympathy with Henry George's noble protest against the industrial oppression of the people. No man believes more firmly than I do that every man has a sacred right to a foothold on the earth. I am not yet qualified to say that the Single Tax is the cure for our social miseries. I have but recently begun investigation. But of one thing you may rest assured, that no production of my pen will ever be inconsistent with the great ideal of justice which is near and dear to your heart. It has done me good to read your ardent and vigorous letter. There are a few men and women scattered abroad throughout the world who are alive with the Social Passion. They are the salt of the earth, they are the hope of social progress. The Holy truth that they are building on the earth will, in coming days, be a sea-wall against the tides of anarchy and disorder. Respectfully yours, Edwin Markham.

"And there for the first time," reported Anita, "I saw the signature that was to close so many precious letters, and grace the fly-leaves of his books."

On May 17 she wrote him again, another four-page letter commenting at length on a *Tribune* interview he had sent to her. One of his replies to the reporter's questions had included a phrase that "kindled her fancy," as she said. This phrase, "If men were wise and brotherly enough," inspired her to write a poem, "If Men Were Wise." The closing paragraph of her four-page epistle confessed her tender age:

> *It may interest you to know that I am writing this letter on my eighteenth birthday. My earnestness evidently led you to believe me older. But my youth does not prevent me from being ardently devoted to the cause of humanity, and I have had wonderful success in my work as a writer and public*

lecturer. I am very pleased to know you, and hope that you will write to me again.

Anita later wrote that one might have expected the headmaster of a private school in Oakland to be highly amused by this "jejune display of cockiness, but I never had any intimation that he did not take me seriously." He liked her prose better than her poetry, but since she wanted to express herself in that form, he very kindly helped her, as he had done dozens of other aspirants.

Their first meeting was at Tremont Temple in Boston, where Markham was to lecture on October 19. A letter from him asked, "[W]here in Boston can I find you? Grant me the pleasure of taking you to the lecture." This date conveniently coincided with her registration at Emerson College of Oratory, and when she received the letter from Edwin Markham, Anita's father suddenly capitulated from his earlier resistance to the idea and decided to come with her. Despite Willie Trueman's prejudice about poets, Markham's fervor on behalf of justice and freedom profoundly impressed him, especially during the lecture at Tremont Temple. "It was such a new experience for Papa to be on the receiving end of a conversation, that my own attention was absorbed by the spectacle. I basked in the aura of my poet, and I was proud of my parent, and of my privilege in bringing them together," Anita wrote.

Then in the prime of his life, Markham made a striking impression, with his flowing white hair and beard, combined with his glowing personality. He told the Truemans about his plan to move east as soon as the child of his marriage—undertaken rather late in life to Catherine, a fellow teacher—was old enough to do so, and invited Anita to call on them when they were settled. In the spring of 1900, she went to their home in Brooklyn, the first of several visits. Catherine Markham became a good friend as well as a gracious hostess, but, as Anita opined:

> *Their way of life was very frugal and their hospitality as measured on the material side as it was large spiritually. There was always a poem in process, and Mrs. M. worked on them with her husband, looking up the classical references and savoring each line as it was written and revised. To be with them in this creative adventure, to listen to the*

*first reading of lines that were to become Literature, made
biscuits and apple sauce and milk seem divine provender.*

Some years later, when Anita took her fiancé, Dr. Robert
Freedman—to whom she was briefly engaged—to meet the Markhams, and the aforementioned menu was served, his annoyance
contributed a great deal toward the dissolution of their engagement.
The honor of meeting the world's most popular poet did not
appease Robert's hunger, especially since, after the long trip to the
Markhams' home on Staten Island, he expected that their supper
invitation indicated "dinner."

During Anita's first visit with them in 1900, Markham had a
caller—a woman who seemed to be in deep mental distress. "Mr.
Markham," she said, "Do you believe the Bible is the word of God?"
Anita writes that he turned his leonine head and gazed out of the
window a full minute before very slowly answering, "I believe the
word of God is *in* the Bible, as a nut is in its shell. You have to crack
the shell to find the nut." The visitor sighed, "I guess I'll join the
Catholic Church, and then I won't have to think about such questions any more."

After Anita's week-long visit in their Staten Island home in
1901, Markham and his son, Virgil, accompanied Anita on the ferry
back to New York:

*Virgil was between us, straining to get out of the window.
Papa, holding on to his skirts, quoted for me a quatrain
which he had written that morning for the baby.*

*'There are three green eggs in a small brown pocket
And the breeze will swing and the gale will rock it,
Till three little birds on the thin edge teeter,
And our God will be glad and our world will be sweeter.'*

The *New York World,* a popular but sensational newspaper in
1899, "kept its hold in the homes of America largely on account of
a short daily editorial, usually in verse, from the pen of Ella Wheeler
Wilcox," according to Anita. This popular poet, who had such an
influence on American households, had been a supporter of Henry
George in his ill-fated campaign, often expressing Single Tax ideas

in her column. The New Haven correspondent for the *World*, who had attended one of Anita's parlor talks, offered to give a luncheon to introduce Anita to Mrs. Wilcox.

The following Sunday, the *New York World* featured Anita's picture and an article quoting Ella Wheeler Wilcox as saying, "The girl is wonderful. There is some divine power back of it all, some great mind of past ages, living again in her." Anita's response was as follows:

> *This was the germ of much newspaper publicity, but it was another challenge to my inner consciousness. I didn't mind being called an "old soul," but in the life-plan illustrated by my center diagram, the soul itself cannot be considered old. It is timeless. What then did my poet-friend mean? Perhaps that I had brought with me into this human life a body of past experience and understanding which could be applied here and now in making my own life richer and my influence more helpful. For by this time I was convinced that I had come into the world to give my message.*

Mrs. Wilcox was evidently mightily impressed with the young girl, for she invited her to go home with her that night of their first meeting. Her home, "the Bungalow," was on the rocky shore at Branford, Connecticut. Anita wrote of that evening:

> *Pausing at home to collect my nightie and report [my] plans, I went with them by trolley and stage to that remote spot. . . . The final stretch of the long journey was made on foot, along a country lane. Finally we emerged at Short Beach, still a remote bit of shore at the head of Boulder Bay, with only the Bungalow for human habitation. . . . Here Robert* [Mrs. Wilcox's husband] *had his retreat from literary palaver, and thousands of extra books and curios were stored. . . . [T]he two rearmost rooms [were] the kitchen and the cat-room. I suspect this had been intended by the architect as a dining-room, but E. W. W. had acquired a large family of Angora cats.*

The greatest charm of the place for me was the wide verandah, spreading round three sides of the house. At each corner hung an aeolian harp, singing softly as the breeze caressed it. This music lulled me to sleep that night, and in the morning, I climbed about the rocks with the friendly cats and kittens. . . . Later I was to own a descendant of the tribe, our beautiful Bruin.

Ella's mother had come to live with them; she was elegantly dressed, with a lace mantilla over her head, but was peevish over being uprooted from her Minnesota farm and made into an artistic figure. At breakfast she complained because the kumquats were not oranges. Finally Ella expostulated with her fretfulness. The old lady bristled, "Well, I'm the way the Lord made me, and if he doesn't like me, he can change me."

When writing her memoir decades later, Anita declared that the memory of that night and morning lingered with her even then, and that it had been not only a thrilling adventure, but the start of a wonderful friendship. It was one of the poet's hobbies to help promising young people, but she and her husband gave Anita not only encouragement but real companionship. When she wrote her verses of tribute to Mrs. Wilcox, it was Robert who had them framed.

At the time of her first meeting with Ella Wheeler Wilcox, Anita was working on a long narrative poem, "Aceon: a Tale of the Soul's Experience." According to her, early infatuations for a musician and a painter were sublimated in this poem, and she said further:

Gleanings from Theosophy seem to have blended with my conviction that our human personality is only a fraction of our self-hood. Emerson's oversoul had become for me a definite individual Self, including the lesser, visible, personal self. A certain surrender of this separate personal Self to the Divine Higher Self, comparable to the orthodox "conversion" is presented as the first step toward At-One-ment with the Oversoul and the Cosmic Universal Spirit.

All this was woven into the tale of two incarnations of Aceon, together with a "canto" expounding the Single Tax. Anita rewrote the poem over and over again, each time sending a copy to some prominent person for criticism. In this way, she acquired some valuable instruction and made some choice friends. Ella Wheeler Wilcox boosted her faith by writing, "Aceon is fine and strong and full of excellence." Other criticisms resulted in many rewritings resulting in the "reduction of redundance," according to Anita. Anita's poem of tribute to Ella Wheeler Wilcox is contained in her book *Aceon,* the printing of which Mrs. Wheeler helped subsidize. When Anita offered to repay part of it, Mrs. Wheeler told her to forget it—that if all young people she helped did as well as Anita, she would be satisfied.

As Anita wrote her autobiography many years later, she mused over another memorable event in 1903 concerning her poet friend: a dinner and reception that the Woman's Henry George League of New York held in honor of Mrs. Wilcox. Anita was one of several illustrious speakers: Catherine Markham (wife of the poet Edwin), feminist author Charlotte Perkins Stetson Gilman, Harriot Stanton Blatch (daughter of Elizabeth Cady Stanton), Henry George, Jr., and others. Anita commented that she was at the head table with all these dignitaries; for once she was not ill at ease socially:

> [A]t the very beginning, my slinky black velvet dress made a great impression. Charlotte Gilman, who was willowy herself [Anita later added that she looked like a Rosetti portrait], pounced on me, and said I should always wear black velvet. The Single Taxers knew me for my work in "the campaign" and in New Haven. The literati knew of me as the girl philosopher, so the pre-gustatory pleasures of the occasion mounted to the point where Ella Wheeler Wilcox herself arrived, and greeted me with delight over my appearance. She herself was gowned in lace over rich yellow, accented by her lovely topaz jewels which shone like her reddish-gold hair. The contrast was immediately noticed as we chatted together....When I stood beside my friend and recited my poem of tribute, she reached out her arm and drew me close to her, a gesture which brought a burst of applause from the audience.

Anita's short-lived association with Emerson College came about as a result of her poem "Aceon" being sent by a New Haven dramatics teacher—with Anita's permission—to the founder of the school, Dr. Charles Wesley Emerson. His response, by letter, commented favorably on the poem and Anita's ability, and in time she received another letter offering her free tuition. Although the demand for her lectures proliferated that winter and following spring, so that she decided not to continue at Emerson, she felt that she had absorbed, under Doctor Emerson's personal direction, what the college had to teach her:

> I had learned to "speak to their minds, not their ears." I had learned to dwell with a picture or a theme in my own mind before trying to present it to an audience. I had acquired the characteristic Emerson posture, and the habit of interpreting any subject with my whole personality.

There she learned a system of physical exercises set to music that became a lifelong practice for tuning up her speaking voice. She was to adopt Emerson's habit of responding to flattery and even honest appreciation with the phrase "Thanks be to the Giver of all Gifts." In her later years, she was claimed as an alumna of the college, by then a full-fledged institution of general learning with emphasis on communications and dramatics, in its own buildings overlooking Boston's Charles River.

While still at Emerson College, Anita had been deeply impressed with a selection called "The Infinite Mother" by James G. Clarke. Edwin Markham's "Song to the Divine Mother" complemented this with the answering cry of the Child. The concept grew within Anita that she, as a human child, could call upon the Divine Mother for strength and wisdom, and that the answer would come through her own "vitalized Center of Being." At other times, she *was* the Divine Mother, directing the Child, and the Voice of the Divine Mother moving creatively in the world among her "hungry-souled companions." "This dynamic dualism was far from being a case of split personality," she wrote, "It gave me a technique for living my peculiar destiny." From that time forward, many of her diary entries were addressed to "Divine Mother."

In her autobiography, Anita reminded her grandchildren that even as she conversed in this spirit of prayer with the Divine Mother, she was quite aware that she was personifying her own inner light, the sacred center within each person that is one with the cosmic life.

While still at Emerson, she attended the Independent Church, which met in a hall in the Pierce Building on Copley Square. It was there that she heard the fiery orator Edward Everett Hale preach, and watched him converse with Helen Keller. Anita described her own meeting with Helen, then a student at Radcliffe:

> I generally sat near her and Anne Sullivan. . . . Anne's rapid fingers transmitted the sermon to the eager spirit of her friend. Being the same age as Helen, and so much interested in speech problems, I was fascinated, and made myself known to them. Anne introduced me, and Helen rapidly read my features with her fingers, placing them on my lips while I spoke, and answering in her high-pitched voice. Then we clasped hands, and the next Sunday she knew me by my hand-clasp.

Barely two weeks after Anita's arrival at Emerson, she received an invitation to address the International New Thought Congress at Lorimer Hall in Boston. In the receiving line at the reception, held in the Mirror Room of the old Parker House, she met many leaders with whose writings she was familiar. She found that they also were familiar with her writing, through reading her essays and poems in various metaphysical magazines: *Mind, The Arena, Kosmos, The Nautilus, Unity,* and others. This occasion—a huge step forward in her career—secured for her a dozen speaking engagements in other cities and a course of lectures in Boston for that winter.

Her presence in Boston that winter was convenient, for she had just gone into the publishing business. In her words, "[i]t had happened in the same fairy-tale manner which characterized so many of my other adventures." Josephine Fuzzard, an enthusiastic admirer of Anita's speech at the convention, asked her what she had written. Anita's admission to having a sheaf of manuscripts, including the poem that had won her the Emerson scholarship, led to an offer of help toward publication. Josephine's financial backing made possible the first printing of five hundred copies of *Philo-Sophia: A Volume of Love-Wisdom Poems,* bound in Yale blue cloth. This first edition sold out quickly, many to fellow Emersonians, and her backer insisted on another edition. This larger version, on larger pages and with two new poems added, carried a gold fleur-de-lis on the blue cover—echoing the blue flannel blouse embroidered with fleur-de-lis that Anita wore all that winter. Anita wrote about the advent of this second edition:

> *I remember the astonishment with which the manager at Gilson's [publishing company] greeted me when I went in to arrange about this second edition. "Well, you are a wonder," he said. "You not only publish books before you are out of short skirts, but you* sell *them." After repaying my friend what I had borrowed, I had a dribble of income from this edition to add to the precarious profits of my lecture work.*

During the Easter recess from Emerson, Anita had speaking engagements in Providence, Rhode Island; in New York City; in Wilmington, Delaware; and at the Circle of Divine Ministry in Washington, D.C. The publicity literature for these events quoted Ella Wheeler Wilcox's review of Anita from the *New York World,* as quoted earlier—"The girl is wonderful. There is some divine power back of it all, some great mind of past ages, living again in her." Anita wrote of this praise:

> *These words . . . had important results in my life. Not only did they attract audiences, and predispose them to listen to me respectfully, but they created a pattern for my own thinking. I have never escaped from the feeling of being very young, and when I spoke with authority, I felt the attitude expressed by Jesus, "It is not I that speak, but the Father that dwelleth in me."*

At her New York stop on this tour, a reporter from the *Evening Telegram* wrote a two-column spread with Anita's picture and the heading "SHE'S REINCARNATED, ALL RIGHT, BUT DENIES THAT SHE'S SOCRATES." Upon her return to Emerson after the vacation tour, she encountered an odd welcome—amusement from some of the students, and stony looks from the teachers. She couldn't understand it until someone showed her the previous Sunday's edition of the *Boston Post,* containing a full-page story, complete with a string of line drawings and a heading that screamed, "PLATO'S SPOOK." The various drawings showed the young philosopher addressing a Washington audience, with senators in the front row, "practicing oratory" with Dr. Emerson calmly observing and cavorting in calisthenic poses. The final drawing was a bust of Plato.

The reporter who wrote the article had fabricated it from the New York papers and from interviews of a skeleton office force during the school vacation. Journalistic license produced this sensational article. Anita's acute embarrassment over this "massive dose of humiliation" produced a psychosomatic illness with fever and visible rash, and she was ordered to be shipped home from Emerson by a doctor who feared it might be scarlet fever. This ended her association with the college, for by then her work was calling her in other directions, and she felt she could not escape from the growing demands on her time.

The Vedanta Influence
and the Peace Flag

Anita's meeting in 1900 with Swami Abhedananda, the head of
the Vedanta Society in America, while not her first exposure to
Eastern philosophy, proved to be pivotal in her spiritual journey.
Her encounter with the swami, who was to become a close friend,
came about when Anita was engaged to speak at a luncheon-lecture
series at the suggestion of Ella Wheeler Wilcox. Florence Guernsey,
daughter of a prominent New York City physician—the head of the
Hahnemann Hospital—arranged entertainments in their apartment
on Central Park South so that her aging mother could participate.
The Guernseys were already interested in Anita from newspaper
articles. Anita wrote about one such lecture:

> *I was wearing the same blue flannel shirtwaist* [with the
> fleur-de-lis] *and black broadcloth skirt which I had been
> wearing at College and on my recent tour. Florence . . . tried
> to robe me in white draperies for the lecture, but after they
> had left me to meditate while they attended to the arriving
> guests, I changed back into the garments which were part of
> my personality, the outfit pictured in so many newspaper
> articles. By this time, syndicates had spread them all over the
> country.*

Anita wrote that she was troubled to learn that Florence was
charging her guests a dollar apiece and wondered who would pay
that much to hear her. But forty of them did, including Mrs.
Hamilton Fish, other society ladies, Ella Wheeler Wilcox, and sev-

eral of her friends. To her surprise, there in the back row was her father, who had come down from New Haven for the occasion. She said, "This was the most disconcerting of all to me. After overcoming the annoyance of my hostess about my clothes, I had to deal with my father's doubt in regard to my mission. But I polarized my being to the divine center within, and let the light flow into my message."

The subject announced was "The Three Orders of Inspiration." As Anita remembered in later years, this lecture was an exercise in spiritual deep breathing, dwelling on the rhythm of one's reactions to one's environment. She proposed that we receive and give, whether we are aware of it or not: that most people are satisfied to react automatically and emotionally in a superficial manner. Anita added that the artist opens his soul to the *inspiration* of nature, people, and experience, and reacts to them in a creative way. The *expiration* in action completes the circuit of one's connection with a higher plane of consciousness. "We can no more receive and hold inspiration than we can keep a lungful of physical air. This deeper breathing of the beauty and meaning of life is the first order of inspiration," according to Anita.

She went on to say that the second order of inspiration follows the same law: that the Master Souls of all time can breathe their spirit into us, if we will lend ourselves to breathing it out again. Her belief was that such souls would never allow us to become mere instruments of their wisdom, that we must guard against letting any lesser beings gain control of us. She suggested that, if there are excarnate spirits with whom we can communicate, even the Master Souls, we must meet them on terms of personal responsibility, breathing the same air.

Anita defined the final and highest order of inspiration as coming from breathing the Cosmic atmosphere to and from the very center of one's being. The disciplines of deep meditation and self control are necessary to the achievement of this degree of consciousness, in which the separate self is merged with the Cosmic Whole.

Swami Abhedananda, in whose beautiful bronze features "the peace of eternity" was seen by Anita, attended only the luncheon, but their conversation began a long association. He had received a copy of her poems. She wrote that she did not remember how she had learned of the Hindu theory of reincarnation, but she had used it in her poem "Aeon" and a couple of shorter poems. It seemed to her to offer a reasonable explanation of the many types of personality, their different degrees of development, and of the seeming injustice and incompleteness of human experience. "It had a place in my Cosmic Scheme," she wrote.

To the high-caste Brahmin Swami Abhedananda, reincarnation was part of his cultural inheritance; since he was deeply versed in the Vedic Scripture, it was the natural framework for his thought. In his philosophy, a nineteen-year-old girl with such a well-established understanding of truth and such a strong sense of mission in sharing it with others must be, as Ella Wheeler Wilcox said, an "old soul." Anita's comment was that they were spiritual comrades from the start.

According to Anita's writings, the swami had become a youthful disciple of Ramakrishna; his Brahminism was tempered with the gospel of his master, "that all religions are true, and every soul must find its own way to the Source of Being." He had succeeded Swami Vivekananda, the senior member of that group of disciples, who had been sent to the Parliament of Religions at the Chicago World's Fair in 1892 to represent Hinduism. Vivekananda's address captured the audience, starting him on a whirlwind tour of America. He found multitudes of unsatisfied souls hungering for his message, and soon there were Vedanta Societies in several large cities. When Vivekananda became ill, he spent his last strength establishing the Ramakrishna Brotherhood, which was to be a powerful force in the awakening of India under Gandhi's leadership, according to Anita. Abhedananda was sent to take his place in America, and, in 1900 when he and Anita met, "my beautiful bronze Hindu," as Anita called him, was head of the Vedanta Society of America.

During the summer following their meeting, they were guests of the Guernseys again, this time at their summer home at Fishkill-on-the-Hudson, New York. Anita commented that fine hospitality and glorious scenery were a good setting for the growth of the friendship that was to mean so much to her through the years. Later that summer, she was giving a course of lectures at Greenacre, Maine, a summer colony and school for advanced thought, when the swami arrived there. Anita told that many of the people were interested in Vedanta, so the coming of the swami made quite a stir.

Some of the old ladies "ached to touch the hem of his tunic," according to Anita, and "almost swooned at the sound of his voice," so they were amazed when after supper he and Anita went walking together.

Anita delighted in hearing his lectures, but her own were still well attended. She wrote that a critical attitude, which she had sensed, notably diminished when the people saw that they were really friends. Her report of that evening is as follows:

> *It was there in the grove of tall pines that we spent an evening in silence, watching the moon climb the sky, and when we rose to go back to the hotel, Swamiji kissed me. It was just so, with no passion, no desire, no regret. The earth and the heavens had given us of their holiest, and that kiss was the seal of a supreme experience. It left no embarrassment in our relationship.*

He never questioned Anita's call to her work, though he sometimes made fun of her seriousness about it, and warned her, as in this letter, of its dangers:

> My dear child, I was extremely delighted to see you here yesterday . . . though it was only for a short time. I am glad to hear that the work you are doing is meeting with such a great success everywhere. . . . Do not be guided by ambition. Do not be puffed up with vanity. . . . Do not think for a moment that it is *your* work, and that these are *your* students. Do not think that you are a teacher. First learn to be a true disciple. No one has ever become the true teacher without becoming a true and faithful disciple of some spiritual master. Even Christ himself had to become a disciple first. . . . You are doing a good work, no doubt, but I know that you are still a child in spiritual life. . . . May Divine Mother bless you.
>
> Abhedananda

Although Anita often expressed self-doubts in her diaries and journals, this is one of the few times that we gain insight into how her early fame may have inflated her vision of herself; her comment, written decades later, was that she needed this reproach and admonition at that time. And how could it not turn the head of such a young woman to be so lionized and quoted in newspapers all over the country? That much attention could make a much older person full of herself. We, as readers of Anita's life story, can recognize and forgive the youthful self-absorption.

Most of Swamiji's letters were addressed, "My dearest and best beloved Sophia," and were warmly solicitous. The device she was using to hold herself together in those days was the concept of the higher and lower selves, the superconscious and the manifest self. She called her inner, higher self Philos, and the outer self Sophia. This explains the title of her volume of poems, and the addressing of his letters to Sophia.

Some years later, Anita had the privilege of living in the Vedanta house one winter, while she was giving lectures for the Liberal Leagues in New York, with long discussions and a rebuttal afterward. It was a great comfort to her to have "that haven of silence, that battery of spiritual force," behind her. Often she would go into Swamiji's study for a few moments of devotions with him before taking up the cudgels with her argumentative audience. She said that Swamiji never failed her, but often he laughed with her over the vanity of all this: "Only those who are detached can see how funny life is. The work of evolution goes on, whether you or I care to push it or not!"

Anita, although not a student as were the other residents, was allowed to rent a room, as a protégé of Abhedananda, in the Vedanta House, a luxurious brownstone on Seventy-Second Street in New York City. She described the "Silent Room" with its sunny altar, where no one spoke at all: above the altar the eye rested upon some symbol of world religion, changed from day to day as the festivals of different faiths appeared on the calendar. Entering this room for meditation, there was always a symbol to guide thought, if needed. Those who had become familiar with the inner light of the spirit seldom left the place without a spiritual greeting to the segment of humanity represented by the day's symbolism.

The Catholicity of Vedanta, as expounded by its modern saint, Ramakrishna, and by the founder of the American Vedanta Society, Vivekananda, was illustrated while she was living there by a celebration of the 2450th anniversary of the birthday of Gautama

Buddha, called the Feast of Mercy. Anita wrote, "[W]e held open house, and for once there was chatter in the Vedanta rooms, as scores of Japanese and other Buddhists came and went. It was salutary to be reminded how much younger our Christian faith is."

The time came when Abhedananda went back to India to spend a season building up the Brotherhood, which was to become the backbone of Gandhi's movement.

In 1901, Anita began an involvement with the Universal Peace Union.[1] She spoke at meetings in Boston, Massachusetts and Mystic, Connecticut. There were interurban trolleys in those days, and she enjoyed the ride from New Haven, little realizing toward what a strange chapter in her life she was traveling.

At this gathering she saw for the first time the Peace Flag, which was to be such a large part of her life. She wrote a history of the flag, saying that in 1891, when it was already twelve years old, there had been a meeting of the Human Freedom League at Independence Hall in Philadelphia, at which a committee was appointed to design a banner to serve as a symbol of peace among nations. A design presented by Henry Pettit was chosen, proposing that each nation simply use its own flag against a white field as a symbol of the dedication of its special values and loyalties to world welfare. The flag would bear a streamer at the top with the words "Peace to all Nations." Anita noted that the first flag was made by American women from silk produced by the American Silk Growers' Union.

There at Mystic, this very flag was displayed. Those in attendance were told that it had been taken to Italy in November 1891 and accepted by a Peace Congress held in Rome, this being confirmed by a Peace Congress held at Berne, Switzerland, in 1892. The guardian of the flag at the Rome Congress was a Mrs. Gillespie, a granddaughter of one of Benjamin Franklin's sixteen brothers and sisters; the banner she displayed showed the American flag set in a white border. Despite anti-American sentiment, Mrs. Gillespie's talk met with complete approval, according to Anita.

After Anita spoke at Mystic, Dr. Robert Samuel Freedman took the floor to express his surprise that in twelve years nothing more had been done with this great idea. He proposed to have several copies of the flag made and presented to public figures, who would popularize the idea. Robert quietly offered to pay for them, thus becoming the angel of the Universal Peace Union "and mine," as Anita added.

A trolley ride home together led to plans to see each other in New York City the following week, and a promise of the first of his new Peace Flags. Anita said, "We felt that we were partners in a great enterprise." Robert, at forty-four twice Anita's age, was a Hungarian Jew. She claimed never to have known what kind of a doctor he was, although they came to be intimate friends and were for a time engaged to be married. All of their mutual interests centered on the Peace Flag.

The story of their brief romance and the Peace Flag continued. When Anita was in New York, he entertained her royally, showering gifts upon her, including a very beautiful black panne velvet coat, lined with white silk. When she was at home, he wrote brief letters, always enclosing a gold piece—usually the tiny half eagle—with suggestions for its use. She wrote, "[H]e wanted a portrait of me, an artistic one, and so I have a record of the famous black velvet dress in its original form." Anita said that after she took up her work with the People's Church in New Haven, some of the little gold pieces were contributions to that cause.

The fact that she was interested in a wealthy man pleased her parents, especially since he was a reformer. On October 11, 1901, he came to New Haven to meet her family. He brought wonderful gifts for all of them—including a tall bottle of champagne, making the event a celebration. Best of all, he brought two Peace Flags, and gave Anita her choice. In one, the field of stars was embroidered in white, the other in gold. She chose the one with white stars; Anita and Robert gave the other to Ella Wheeler Wilcox, who was quite interested in their romance.[2]

On December 10, the engagement was announced by Anita's parents and, in spite of her request for a simple engagement ring, Robert sent by registered mail a band with three diagonally set diamonds. Anita's comments were that each of the diamonds was larger than any she had ever seen in an engagement ring and that she hesitated to wear it in public—that the possession of it caused her constant anxiety: "I never was meant for luxury."

After a visit to Robert's family, who considered Anita unsuitable, and with growing discomfort at sharing the stage with him in the great social events he planned, she knew the engagement was a mistake, much as she enjoyed pursuing the Peace Flag project with him. Her parents were shocked and disappointed at her decision not to marry him, but she said: "I am sure Robert was as much relieved as I." Although her telling of this story in her autobiography was somewhat cavalier, a later entry reveals that she became so ill after breaking the engagement that she had to relinquish her position as associate minister at the People's Church in New Haven. According to Anita, before this decision was reached, the huge Peace Flags arrived from the factory, and when Robert unpacked them—one American and one British—he draped them about Anita by way of a private dedication. He then took them to Washington to present them to the Dutch embassy for use in the Peace Palace at The Hague. They were blessed by Cardinal Gibbons and used at the first meeting of the International Parliamentary League, held in the Executive Chamber of the Capitol. They were exhibited before a joint session of Congress before being sent on their way. Another of the flags was exhibited at the St. Louis World's Fair. Anita gave Peace Flag talks in public schools, in churches, and at New Thought Conventions. For her grandchildren she wrote:

You will find among my clippings a picture of me and my Peace Flag taken at the People's Industrial College. It pleased me, many years later, to see a picture of Lincoln Center, our Unitarian Settlement House in Chicago, with the Peace Flag flying above its roof. I had helped to put it there.

An enlarged portrait of Anita with the Peace Flag resides in the Unitarian Universalist Heritage room at Rowe Camp and Conference Center in the Berkshire Mountains of Western Massachusetts (see frontispiece). This room, dedicated in December 1993 as a repository for Unitarian Universalist history documents and a reading library, honors Anita's contribution toward the founding of Rowe Camp during the years that she served as summer minister there—her first parish after her ordination in 1921.

Inspiration for
Nature Writing

In 1903, Anita spent some time with her friend Lora Snyder in West Park, New York. Before meeting John Burroughs, the Catskill Mountains' ultimate naturalist and author of twenty-seven books of nature essays, she went to Slabsides, his rustic cabin. It was here that he did his writing and entertained such friends as Henry Ford, John Muir, Harvey Firestone, Theodore Roosevelt, and Thomas Edison, as well as groups of Vassar girls, in whose company he delighted. Her July 30 diary described the visit:

This is the rustic home of John Burroughs, the heaven of birds. I think the birds have religions, and one of them teaches that there is a heaven, where the souls of good birds go, to hold communion with the great Lover of Birds, a place which he has prepared for them. He is away just now, but the cottage, like a nest among the trees, is redolent of the fragrance of his personality. We wandered over here this morning and appropriated the place. We went through the Emerson system of physical culture here on the porch, and then spent a few minutes in meditation. Lora has gone on home leaving me to enjoy the sanctity and beauty of the place alone. Below me, here in the sunlight, spreads the famous celery patch,[1] its bright green obscuring the rich black earth of the ancient lake-bed. Here only the sighing wind and the songs of birds are heard.

While lecturing in Kingston, New York, at the Sahler Sanitarium, Anita went with Lora to West Park, hoping to finally meet John Burroughs. Her diary recorded their first meeting, on August 17, 1903, when she stopped at the post office:

> *There he was, my poet who was to become such a dear companion through the years. He had heard about my preaching and was a little quizzical, for his own religion was extra mural* [sic], *but he invited me to come with Lora to Slabsides the next day.*

When they visited him again on August 18, he spoke with tender feeling of Whitman. "To him," Anita said, "the man was index to the book, and he cannot see how one not having known the man personally can know his soul as I do." He gave her a photograph of the "good gray poet," taken in Whitman's last days, that Anita treasured as a memento of this visit.

Throughout Anita's life, she would draw comfort from Whitman's phrase, "Ebb, Ocean of Life, the flow will return," seeming to take courage from it even when, as in 1956, she accompanied it by writing "The feeling of depression with undertones of grief and guilt persist." Of Burroughs she wrote:

> *I wish I might see more of him since he finds so much pleasure in our friendship. We were boy and girl together yesterday. He told me much of birds and trees, and took me to wonderful secret places in the woods. . . . a place to awaken holiness in the heart, and to cement the companionship of artist-souls. Back at Slabsides we prepared a delightful lunch and "kept house" in truly bohemian fashion. It was indeed a precious day for both of us.*
>
> *September 25, 1903—This has been the richest of many days. . . . I wandered down to where the study nestles under the crest of the hill, overlooking the Hudson. There I found the dear old man, among a disorderly pile of books and papers. He was delighted to see me. . . . He is evidently deeply interested in me. How fortunate I am to have such friends really care for me.*

Anita completed the saga of that day spent with John Burroughs by saying that they returned to Slabsides, where they built a fire on the wide hearth, then watched the blaze in alternate talk and silence. The poet told the history of his poem "Waiting," which he had written when he was twenty-five. He wrote out a copy of it for her, on his rustic table, while she watched and tended the fire.

Many years later, Anita would write in her autobiography of how that autographed copy of the classic verses became valuable to her family in an unusual way when her children were growing up. A representative of the Grolier Society called one day hoping to interest her in *The Book of Knowledge.* This was the first of the Children's Encyclopedias, comprehensive and fascinating to Anita. However, it was quite beyond her means. The agent settled for conversation and a cup of tea. In the course of their talk, Anita bragged about her associations with writers of the previous decade, and showed the saleswoman this copy of "Waiting."

A few days later, Anita received a letter from the Grolier Society, offering her a set of *The Book of Knowledge,* if she would take it in exchange for the manuscript copy of Burroughs's famous poem. They were presenting a deluxe edition of Burroughs's works to a Beacon Hill dignitary, and would like to include the writer's autograph. Anita wrote, "[O]f course I could not consider giving up my treasure, but I wrote 'Oom John' about the offer. He sent me a copy written on fine parchment, which delighted the donors. Meanwhile the precious twenty volumes bound in blue buckram came to our house to stay, and I am sure the fancier later editions and all the modern beauties have never been used as constantly and heartily as these."

Her diary excerpts indicated that Burroughs treasured their time together as much as Anita did, despite the vast difference in their age: she was in her early twenties and he in his late sixties. These entries also gave insight into the moods and feelings of his later life:

> *Yesterday . . . I found him suffering from an aching head, and very sad. He grows weary of the endless procession of people that pass him by, or press around him, without answering his heart's cry for comradeship. I cannot tell why he should love me so, but yesterday he seemed to need me*

51

very much. I cured his headache for him, and he seemed to find balm for his sorrows in my companionship. He still keeps my books on his table, and talks kindly of me to our mutual friends.

A midnight entry in her diary told of how one beautiful gift of three of John Burroughs's books, sent with a letter, made that day "rich beyond measure" for Anita:

His love for me almost makes me sad. Few people have ever loved me as he does. In spite of all his popularity, he is cruelly alone in these days of his old age, that ought to run so smoothly. He needs affection as much as I do. Yet so much stands between us. It is the old story: "You shall not allow the hold of those who stretch their reached hands toward you." But I am very glad to have made a few of his days a little happier, and I hope there may be many more visits to and fro in the coming years. Make our comradeship wholly a blessing to both of us, dear Mother.

May it not be that from such hours of close companionship, something of his large, tender spirit may enter into my being, and pass to those who will not have the opportunity of knowing him as I do? It is a gift, a privilege . . . which I treasure. . . . I am coming to see more and more that I must not deprive myself of experiences which so enrich my life, for any conventional reasons.

Anita wrote of a moonlight walk they took together, saying that the High Road was more picturesque than ever before. "I have tramped it alone . . . but last night there was all the peace of solitude, and all the joy of companionship aglow in our hearts. The world was young, and we two came down from the hills, fully aware of the beauty about us."

Anita accompanied "Oom John" to East Orange, New Jersey, to try to locate the school where he had taught during the Civil War. She wrote an article about this for the *Newark Evening News,* later reporting that she was paid in cash and in a letter from Oom John, beginning, "Thank you for sending me the little sketch. The sketch was cleverly done, and gave me much pleasure." She revealed that all of this delving into the past was very painful to Burroughs. Several times he voiced the most profound sadness to think that, as he said, "Life lies behind me now. How willingly I would burn my books and my house and relinquish all I have, to be young and poor again." Anita found it necessary to talk quite seriously to him of the ideals that make life serene and sweet to so many souls. He responded brightly, called her his little philosopher, and seemed his true self again.

Eighty years later, Burroughs's granddaughter and biographer, Elizabeth Burroughs Kelley, would write in a letter that she was glad to learn of this important chapter in her grandfather's life; that she wished she had known of this friendship, which obviously meant so much to him, when writing his biography. She wrote that it was obvious to her why the friendship was neglected by his biographer Dr. Clara Barrus, author of four books about John Burroughs, saying that "Burroughs was never complimentary if he thought Dr. Barrus would be jealous." In Mrs. Kelley's rewrite of *John Burroughs' Slabsides,* she included two paragraphs on Anita.

The night before the aforementioned trip to East Orange, New Jersey, Burroughs went to New York City to hear Anita speak and commented, "Miss Trueman's lecture was not calculated to interest a miscellaneous audience. It was profound, but unrelieved by any glint of humor or vivacity. But the demon sleepiness possessed me that night and I was in agony most of the time and followed her but poorly. Her talk was tinged by the so-called New Thought, and was calculated to take better with some minds than with mine."

Anita's friendship with Burroughs and her own nature writing peaked during those early years before her marriage. In addition to the considerable influence of Burroughs, much of Anita's inspiration came from the beauty of the mighty Hudson River. She wrote of taking the Hudson River Day Line steamer the *Mary Powell,* much-loved "Queen of the Hudson," to New York City from Kingston:

The day is yet young and maiden-shy. . . . The wooded slopes of yonder mountain whisper across the blue air, of the wonderful comradeship which they have fostered. What romance and tragedy those hills have meant to me!

When I stole out of the house this morning, the hush of dawn was still upon the earth. The streets of Kingston were silent, the shades of the houses drawn like the closed lids of sleepers. The air was mountain-sweet, and my lungs expanded unconsciously to their full capacity. Presently. . . . The branches were alive with the songs of birds. One broad lawn was all a-glitter with dew.

Her description of a gorgeous moonlit early morning rain reads, "The very taste of it all became part of my being. Never again shall I be the same, since that beauty has entered into me."

She explained to her grandchildren, in her autobiography, what purpose these writings served to the young Anita: that they were the anodyne for her youthful miseries. "How often they tided me over actual crises," she wrote. Further philosophy blends with her descriptions of nature in these passages:

Only moral relationships are confusing. Nature's great heart beats always near to mine. Her kind face comforts me. Her dramatic moods entertain and inspire me. . . . We are all one stream, which as it descends through the channels of expression, splits into many rills, each individual, yet part of the Whole. . . . Such gifts Nature offers her children, and are they not worth a few moments of attention?

. . . Last night we left the embers of a glorious fire glowing on the hearth to steal out and see the hunter's moon, now in the full. . . . The earth itself seemed potent with strange energies under that dominant moon. Some commanding Power seemed to call forth all the fays and fauns and fairies of the hills, and bid them revel as in olden days, unmindful of the invasion we mortals have made upon their domain. But you, dear spirits of these rocks and trees, you must admit me to your fellowship, for I love you and your haunts as few mortals do. Tell me your secrets and I'll bless you in return. . . . O Camerado, what joy this is!

Anita wrote in her autobiography that such communings with her inner self, in her journal, "corrected the agitation of my human mind, and sometimes brought forth practical solutions for my problems." She added that her fellowship with nature fed her spiritual being, and enabled her to bear trials.

> *It seemed to me that without love the beauties of Nature are vacant and speechless. There is a ravishing beauty in the night when we wander with some dear one. The closer the companionship, the more eloquent Nature seems. But this passionate loveliness sung by the poets passes into insignificance when compared with the majestic splendor of night when I wander alone under its azure canopy, star-gemmed, seeking communion with the Infinite. The larger our love, the greater is Nature's message for us.*
>
> *There are times when the sky is black, and the earth mere dust heaped in a hundred shifting forms. That is when I am selfish and forget my mission in the world. O calm advancing moon, teach me thy lessons of patience and constancy. O wide, tender sky, teach me thy beneficence and breadth. O luxuriant trees, breathing the high airs of heaven, and bathed in the exquisite light of the soaring moon, let me absorb your spirit of stability and aspiration. O Mother Divine, teach me all virtues, that I may serve Thee well among Thy children.*

A frequent companion on her nature walks, the *Journal Intime* of Henri Amiel, Swiss lay theologian, inspired the following paragraphs concerning the role of a journal in Anita's life:

> *Today I have been reading the journal of Henri-Frederic Amiel. . . . Amiel's whole life and death is a great spiritual drama, although his external life seemed so weak and unfruitful. . . . He could not be the companion, so he created what seems almost like a soul itself, the Journal, to speak for him. So you, Camerado, shall speak for me. You shall be the companion of my soul in these coming days. You shall be the Voice of God and Nature, interpreting for me the meaning of my experiences. You shall reflect my deepest thoughts*

and record my dreams. You shall travel with me into new fields, and visit many homes that are being prepared for us.

The Hudson River, seen either from the shore or from the deck of the *Mary Powell,* served as muse for this most eloquent passage in her diary:

The splendor grows. Half an hour ago, I thought the sunset over, but now its glory deepens and every cloud in the heavens reflects it. Away to the north, long, horizontal bars of blue cross the gold. In the southwest, billowy clouds glow with delicate rosy hues. The flag at the prow is dropped. The day is done.

A moment now for my dear ones everywhere. Dear River, flowing southward, carry my love to my comrades in the Metropolis. Dear breeze, blowing from the northwest, if you find my home in your course, whisper words of love to my dear ones there. Dear sun, going westward, before you set over the cities I love, bless my companions there, and bid them think of me. Fair moon, as you sail across the heavens this night, speak to all who love me, and tell them I carry them all in my heart.

You shall hold the record, little book. You shall recall the image when its elements have dissolved. Others will row in the same boat upon the Hudson. Even now, perhaps, the same oars are in other hands, that I swept thru the resisting water. I love all who shall share the Hudson with me, in the coming years, and all who have absorbed its beauty in the past. You, Camerado, whoever you are, I love you.

Anita continued to keep journals and diaries throughout her lifetime. In her seventies, she began Volume XV of her journal by commenting that she caught from Amiel the idea of using such a recording as an alter ego, probably the primary purpose in most journals. She continued, saying that, when there are problems to be faced and spiritual battles to be fought, the soul retreats from companionship, and finds in written ruminations and prayer a relationship with the eternal. Or on common days, for one who is living alone, as she was, it is pleasant to read over a mere catalog of the day's small events, or a description of yesterday's sunset, just as one reads over a letter before mailing it.

While staying in Washington, she wrote that on a "day for dreams," when a wild storm of wind and driving rain prevented an anticipated country drive, she had been idle—reading and talking. From her window, she could see the splendid square pile of the Library of Congress, surmounted by its gilded dome. She proudly observed that within those walls were her books, copies of her play, and records of her copyrights. She wrote that, in days to come, readers might sit under that dome, reading her books. "For who is better equipped for this writing of books,—books of deep human experience? And if the gift of language has been mine for the work of the platform, shall it not also be mine for the writing of books?"

I shall build, during the summer, a book which shall embody what I have learned through my own suffering and sympathy, of that new type of woman whom the world so little understands. She is pre-eminently the mother, yet she is nearly always cut off from human motherhood by the very fact that she is too large-minded, too mighty-hearted, too creative and positive, to be loved by a mortal man. In the present order, she is abnormal. She is ahead of her time. She is the sacrifice needed to bridge over one era to another in the world's history. When the new order is established, our grand-daughters ought to have some record of the revolution which brought them liberty. And the present day needs this study of one of its most characteristic productions.

Anita emphasized that a love of nature was one strong feature of this woman. She said, "I can make a good story of it all, too. But I have not yet found a title for it." She wrote, near the end of her life, that not a word of it was ever written, saying that it was strange that with her ambition to write, some ability, and much encouragement from journalist and literary friends, she failed to find a place in that field:

The Spoken Word, after all, was my natural medium of expression, and delivering it engaged my whole being. It flowed through my mind, voice and body, like an irresistible stream. Yet I was well aware that the Divine Mother, to whom I prayed, was truly my own inner being, that Center through which I was related to the whole Cosmos. I could write down a lecture after I had given it, but not before. That certain audience determined its content and form. They were part of my very life.

I verily believe that there is a spiritual continuum in which we are all bathed and which we can use if we are aware of it. So in speaking I have always felt that my audience became a living organism as responsive to me as nerve ganglia are to the brain. Some would be so active that I gathered inspiration from them and others called out special answers to their needs. How many times after a lecture or sermon I have looked into eager eyes, and heard the question, "How did you know just what I needed?"

Public Life as a New Thought Preacher

Besides her more intimate friendships, already chronicled, Anita spoke of meeting other people of renown: Ralph Waldo Trine, William James, and Charlotte Perkins Gilman, authors; Elbert Hubbard, author and founder of the American Arts and Crafts Movement; Clarence Darrow, lawyer; William Jennings Bryan, orator; Clara Barton, founder of the American Red Cross; Richard LeGalliene, poet; Carry Nation, temperance advocate; Elizabeth Cady Stanton, Susan B. Anthony, and Belva Lockwood, suffragists; Alexander Graham Bell, inventor; Emma Goldman, avowed anarchist; Antoinette Brown Blackwell, first woman to be ordained in the United States; and William Beebe, naturalist-ornithologist. Additionally, she told of meeting people whose names are familiar because of their inventions, such as Louis Waterman of fountain pen fame and Joseph Fels, inventor of Fels-Naptha soap. James Hare, the first American war photographer, was her father's close friend, and she worked for a time for Dr. Charles Brodie Patterson, the great psychologist and leader of the New Thought movement. The interchange of ideas with many of these fine minds served as stimulation and education for this young woman.

The stories of meeting these famous folk of the early part of the century found their way into her autobiography—sometimes in brief mention, sometimes in longer anecdotes.

While addressing the Central Labor Union of the District of Columbia in 1902, Anita met and talked with the grand old man of the Labor Union Movement, Samuel Gompers. She commented that the audience was a challenging one, but her memory dwelt on the few moments of conversation with Gompers.

In Washington, D.C., she spoke at a peace meeting in one of the large churches. Speakers on this program were peace activists and suffragists May Wright Sewall, Clara Barton, and Belva Lockwood (first woman admitted to practice law before the U.S. Supreme Court and candidate for the presidency in 1884 and 1888), among others. She says that the older women, especially Clara Barton, were touched by her enthusiasm, expressing their satisfaction at leaving their work to be carried on by a new generation. She deplored in her later writing: "Alas! How we have failed them!"

Not all of Anita's encounters with famous people were positive ones. She told of speaking at the Manhattan Liberal Club in 1905, and after her lecture there seemed to be a conspiracy to discredit her, with one of the speakers coming to the platform amid rousing applause. Anita had suggested that one method of securing freedom is to flow with the tide, to seek fields of agreement rather than to exploit differences. With this the other speaker heartily disagreed, and most of the audience with her. Anita reported that she did recover some support during her rebuttal, but the unknown speaker had stolen the show. "I did not know it then, but she was Emma Goldman."

In Shawnee, Oklahoma, where she had gone in 1904 for two months—the people who invited her assured her it was virgin field for her work—she was scheduled to give a course of lectures in the offices of the Warner Brothers, successful osteopaths. One of their patients, Carry Nation, a militant champion of orthodoxy as well as temperance, roundly condemned them for consorting with the devil.

Anita met Clarence Darrow, who Anita said was a political power to be reckoned with and "much more of a gentleman than I had expected." She also met feminists Dr. Anna Howard Shaw and Susan B. Anthony, when Anthony was eighty years old and soon to fade out of the reform picture. Anita wrote that she gathered inspiration from having touched Anthony's hand.

Her encounters with the famed orator William Jennings Bryan came about after she had given a course of lectures on "The Evolution of Individuality" at the People's Church in New Haven in 1903. She was invited to dine with the minister, Alexander Irvine, and his wife, whose guests were Bryan and Mrs. Bryan, en route to see Count Leo Tolstoy in Russia. Anita commented that Bryan was still a great figure—at close quarters his personality was overwhelming. There was a large crowd waiting to see him at the church where he had promised to speak to the Boys' Clubs. At first, Anita thought she might have to sacrifice her scheduled lecture for that evening, but was persuaded to give it as announced. She had just begun "How to Cultivate a Powerful Personality" when there was a commotion at the rear of the church and in came Bryan followed by the crowd, filling the church:

> *It was a thrilling experience for me. It was amusing that the foremost living example of my subject was there in my audience, and it released my mind and tongue so that there was a dynamic unity of spirit. Afterward, my father introduced himself, and he loved to tell afterward how Mr. Bryan asked "Is that girl your daughter?" and he replied, "I'm her father."*

Upon Bryan's return from Russia, he spoke again for the People's Church at the Hyperion Theatre. By this time, Anita had become the principal platform exponent of the Peace Flag. His subject was "The Prince of Peace," and Anita was there to exhibit and explain the idea of the white-bordered flag.

Antoinette Brown Blackwell, the first woman to be ordained in America, was conducting a service at the Unitarian Church in Elizabeth, New Jersey, when Anita was asked to supply preach there. Anita recalled going home with her after church and meeting Blackwell's daughter's family. When Blackwell asked Anita how many years she had been preaching—her answer was six—Blackwell replied that for her it was sixty. The Reverend Blackwell remained a minister until the age of ninety, serving the Elizabeth church; Anita had an exchange of letters with her for some years.

For one memorable summer in 1905 Anita was in residence at Charles Brodie Patterson's New Thought Summer School. Dr. Patterson—a psychologist, author, lecturer, healer—was the genius of this Summer Institute at Oscawanna, near Peekskill, New York. It was here that Anita met Elizabeth Cady Stanton of suffragist fame; her daughter, Harriot Stanton Blatch; and Ralph Waldo Trine, author of *In Tune with the Infinite,* who became an important influence in Anita's spiritual journey, as well as a dear friend. In fact, a later review from the *Buffalo Courier* said, "Ralph Waldo Trine would describe her as centered in the Infinite."

During the fall following that summer at Oscawanna, Dr. Patterson hired Anita to help him with his burgeoning office work in connection with a new magazine he was launching. She did much of the editorial work on it and wrote a report of the summer's work for *Mind* magazine, in addition to answering the mail. In the winter the offices were in New York City. While she was there as acting secretary, a fascinating gentleman caller came to see Dr. Patterson, who was away at the time. He was rather small, with an impressive white beard, sparkling eyes, and a friendly manner. When he mentioned his name, Anita was thrilled—he was Alexander Graham Bell. The Bell system was young then, and telephones relatively scarce. It was not so much his achievements in that field as his father's invention of "visible speech" that held her attention in their brief conversation. At Emerson College, the students had studied this method and used it as a sort of phonetic shorthand. Also, while working in New York that winter, Anita gave a series of nine lectures and a special course on "The Path to Realization" in the Alliance Metaphysical Rooms.

When Anita made her first visit to Byrdcliffe Art School in Woodstock, New York, she again met author Charlotte Perkins Gilman. She described the encounter:

> *A lovely spot, called Faerygarde by the artists, is covered with a wild blue flower, called bugloss, which seems to have caught the azure of summer skies. Wild red lilies, yellow daisies and white, and a myriad other flowers, bloom among the grasses, and woo the passing winds and vagrant butterflies. Here we found the great woman poet and philosopher, whom I had met at the Wilcox dinner, Charlotte Perkins Stetson Gilman. We found her correcting proofs of a new book, and sat with her under the trees, while she read two chapters of it to us.*

Anita's poem "Aceon" and her book *Anton's Angels* prompted a letter from Dr. R. M. Bucks, one of Walt Whitman's literary executors, who had developed a theory of cosmic consciousness to account for the superbeings who have from time to time appeared in human form—Whitman being a prime example of this to Bucks. His letter reads, in part:

> Dear Miss Trueman, . . . I was much struck by "Aceon." . . . I think I was even more pleased with *Anton's Angels.* . . . I believe you are still quite young. If so I should have great hope that you will reach the Brahmin Splendor. At all events, I know that you are on the narrow path that leads to it, though "many are called, few chosen." I want you to think of me as your friend, R. M. Bucks.

Anita wrote in her autobiography that she had no regrets about not reaching "the Brahmin Splendor." She added that she revered it in others, and knew that she had tasted it herself. In later years, she had the opportunity to talk with author William James when he came to the Picketts' home in Cambridge. He was then working on his book *Varieties of Religious Experience.* He, too, felt that her work had been an example of cosmic consciousness.

In 1902, her first visit to the upstate community that would be her family's home for many years and her retirement home at the end of her life came about as a result of an invitation to give lectures at the Sahler Sanitarium in Kingston, New York. Dr. Charles Oliver Sahler had been a general-practice physician in the Catskill Mountains, when he discovered the beneficial effects of mental suggestion on his cases. He then learned all that science could teach about mental therapeutics and physical therapy, becoming an authority on these subjects. He founded the Sahler Sanitarium based on his newfound knowledge of metaphysics and holism in medicine.

A brochure from that time period shows the kindly, bearded doctor on the front. Inside, together with pictures of several buildings, the text reads:

THE DR. C. O. SAHLER SANITARIUM,
A private institution for the treatment
of Mental, Nervous and Functional disorders by the
PSYCHO-THERAPEUTICAL METHOD OF TREATMENT.

"Turkish, Russian and Electric Cabinet Baths, and all forms of Electrical Treatment" are listed. The brochure tempts with lists of such attributes as pure water, steam heat, parlors, sun parlors, large halls, gymnasium and amusement hall, art and craft workshop, lectures, moving pictures, library, pool and billiard room, large verandas, private seven-acre park, tennis, croquet, fresh milk, cream, eggs, poultry, vegetables, fruit supplied from two large farms, and invigorating air, magnificent scenery, and delightful walks. A line at the bottom says, "No insane cases received."

Anita, never strong—suffering from chronic anemia and recurring depression—and her mother, a later convert, were helped by the visits to the Sanitarium. Anita maintained a connection with the "San" for over 20 years, even going there for her confinement at the birth of her first daughter, Estelle. During her second visit, this time with her mother, an entry in young Anita's diary tells of a visit to Dr. Sahler's farm in Kyserike—on the then-new Ulster and Delaware Railroad. Anita wrote eloquently of the trip:

> *Strange to think that here this genius spent his boyhood. The secret of his large-mindedness is in the sweep of these hills against the sky. Here he practiced for years. He knows every family in the whole region. The plod of his horse's hoofs over these roads, storm and sunshine, day and night was a familiar and welcome sound. There is the echo of Nature's many voices in his life. Thank God that he heard and answered them in those early days. I have seen enough of this country to begin to love it with fervor. I shall return, dear hills and roads and fields. Do not forget me.*

Anita told of a costume party at the Sahler San (advertised as "The San of Don't You Worry") that made her realize as never before how lacking in everyday fun and occasional hilarity her life had been. Any kind of party in her family "had a *purpose* in it—some reform to further. To be gay or jolly just for fun seemed frivolous." In a diary entry from 1903, she expressed her pain over some criticism she had received, yet was grateful for its lesson:

> *Mother Divine, I thank Thee for the lesson I have learned this day through the ministry of criticism. . . . I have been reminded once again of the unattractiveness of my personal-*

ity by the criticism of one of my new comrades. How little there is in me to love, after all! I am the most ungracious, tactless, and ponderous of mortals. No one cares for me who cannot meet me in the work or on the spiritual plane. I am forever putting myself in a false light by inopportune remarks and lack of courtesy. They say that I put a barrier between myself and others. I who love each life I touch so dearly!

Ah, little girl, I have neglected you terribly. Poor, stunted little woman, you have been so starved that only for the work's sake do you exist. It is wrong. For your own sake you shall be lovable. You shall be wholesome throughout, a royal woman in yourself, and so a more perfect vehicle of truth. We are learning this lesson slowly. If it costs time and effort, and even retirement from the work, I must have the rounded character that is my ideal. I must be richly, sweetly personal. I must pour my love into tender, visible companionship.

A few months later, a friend gave her this advice. "You have a marvelously analytical mind. There lies your work. It means aggression. Don't be afraid of it. Don't waste time in diplomacy. Formulate your faith and declare it with authority, and fight for it." "Prepare the way for my feet, and my feet for the way," was Anita's prayerful response. In her last years, she professed that she had been keenly aware of the dangers of vanity and ambition; the journals of those years held pages expressing profound dejection over her failures. She had so wanted her personality and speech to be a pure instrument for the spiritual understanding she felt she could radiate from the divine center within, where she felt a dynamic unity with the Cosmic Spirit and its creative order. "But too often," she said, "I 'came downstairs' into the very kitchen of gossip and criticism and silly vanity."

So thoroughly did she leave this public life behind her—when later she chose marriage and motherhood—that there came a time when her son, Trueman, looking over some of her old letters, said, "Why the deuce don't you keep acquainted with some of these famous people, so there'd be some chance for the rest of us to know somebody worthwhile?" Her literary aside was "Why, indeed? Partly because 'the rest of us' require my time and attention."

In 1904, on Easter Sunday, she agonized over the difficulty of being a "Free Thought" preacher, without the backing and the trappings of the mainstream churches, and prayed for strength:

> *Mother Divine, be with me this coming day, in the work that awaits me. I have the hardest work before me of any minister in the city. The others have flowers and music, and the faith of their congregations in the mystery of the Resurrection and its meaning to them. But I have only my faith in Thee. My people lack that sweet and simple faith which is found in the other churches. They are but a flock gathered in from the wayside having no shepherd. Gather them in, dear Mother, and speak thy word of Truth to their sweet spirit of universal love. Bless me, thy servant, in my ministry among them. Strip me of all vanity and ambition, that in my whole being I may glorify Thee.*

She confirmed her belief in her calling in this prayer:

> *O Mother Divine, I should sink down discouraged, if I alone were to undertake the work that must be done here. But with Thee all things are possible. It hath pleased Thee at this time to call me to this work, and Thou wilt direct and strengthen me in it. I trust it and all else wholly to Thee.*

Always an avid reader, despite weak astigmatic eyes, Anita told of having a special carrying case for books, lined with velvet and covered with tan leather. It held the two dozen volumes that she carried, by hand, everywhere she went. She indulged in dreaming of scholarship—that she might know sciences and languages—but admitted that she might better serve the needs of the people without such knowledge, thinking that it might carry her work beyond their reach. She comforted herself with the hope that the future would bring her a companion whose scholarship would unlock the door of learning for her. "Where are you now, Camerado? I hail you. May we meet soon."

Anita's single years were not without romantic entanglements, but oftener than not, they did not measure up to the "cosmic romance" she sought. Her writings mention various episodes of intimate friendships, unrequited romantic love, or the attention of the following men: John Frederic Mueller, a Buffalo lawyer in his forties; Eugene Heffley, a pianist who was the moving spirit and main support of the (composer Edward) MacDowell Association; Isaac Withers, the composer and publisher of the "Anita Waltzes" (with a picture of our Anita on the cover); a Hungarian portrait painter whom she identified only as Keszthelyi; Bertram Nelson, a young instructor and lay preacher from the University of Chicago; Francis Lathrop, the creator of the altar painting and chancel windows for Saint Bartholomew's Church in New York City, then in his fifties; Major George Geiss, a serious suitor who proposed marriage if Anita would join him in California; Dr. Robert Freedman, the physician to whom she was briefly engaged; Eugene Horton, a friend from Washington; Haswell Jeffries, a friend from New York and Oscawanna; and a few unnamed suitors—most of them unwelcome. A woman friend, Carolyn Rapelje, with whom Anita had started to build a house at Oscawanna, proved difficult: John Burroughs wrote in his diary that Carolyn seemed to be in love with her, to Anita's annoyance, and that "Miss R. lost her lover years ago and seems to have transferred her affections to Miss T." Anita may not have recognized the intensity of her friend's feelings, but was forced to end their housing arrangement because of Carolyn's instability and tendencies to control her.

At one point, having suffered several disappointments in love, she seriously considered—at her father's suggestion—having a deliberate single motherhood. She recorded her thoughts concerning that venture:

Why must I wait 'til the man comes who will share life and the work with me? Why must I wait for my motherhood until I find the conventional conditions congenially provided? Why must a woman barter her freedom for the privilege of motherhood? I'm growing to scorn conventions for their cruelty to women, and I feel the blood of heroes in my veins.

Anita was at an age—early twenties—that found most women of that time already married and having families. She had conflicting feelings about marriage. In one diary entry, after writing about a couple of marriage proposals that didn't please her, she mused:

Strange that I am always haunted by love that I must not accept, devotion that is almost repulsive to me, while the few men I could love turn elsewhere and leave my heart empty.

Dear Mother Divine, I trust all things with thee. Am I to be the voice of a new freedom? . . . for the sake of all unrealized motherhood, for the sake of truth and love and freedom, this thing must be done. I am ready, it is thy will, dear Mother, to place all in the balance. Make me brave enough to support my convictions, and if the conditions are not complete, grant me patience to wait.

When the man whom she had chosen to father this child—Ernest Loomis, a friend and companion from Oscawanna whose wife's invalidism prevented him from enjoying the parenthood he craved—lost courage and withdrew, she consoled herself with thoughts of her calling:

I must go back to the work, the work I came into the world to do. There alone is peace, and real self-expression for me. All other associations deny me and fling me back to the path from which I'm so prone to wander. O Mother Divine, make thy way plain to me, and guide me on the path.

The path seemed to be leading her to Pennsylvania; the work seemed to be calling her to Unitarianism. The Reverend Mason, the Pittsburgh minister and trustee of Meadville Theological School in Pennsylvania,[1] offered to arrange for her to give some lectures there under a fund bequeathed for sociological instruction in the seminary. Anita agreed that if this could be arranged, she would avail herself of the opportunity. According to her, Mason wanted her to be ordained as a minister of the Unitarian Church, and take one of several positions which he thought might be available. One was the Educational Secretaryship of the American Unitarian Association Society at Large, which would mean traveling all over the country and nourishing the mother spirit in Unitarian churches. Then there were traveling professorships, or the possibility of a church of her own. He had no doubt of her fitness for those positions, and Anita promised him that if this proved to be the path for her, she would come to him and his church for ordination. In some ways this seemed to be the answer to the growing needs of her life—stability and security. She wrote, "[A]ll that I wish to do and be, can be done on that foundation, and in some fields the prestige of the church and the co-operation of its leaders would be of great assistance."

While lecturing and preaching extensively at such diverse places as the People's Church in Philadelphia; the Metaphysical Club in Boston; Roycroft in Aurora, New York; the Sahler Sanitarium in Kingston, New York; various Liberal Leagues; the People's Institute Clubs; the Circle of Divine Ministry in Washington, D.C.; and the School for New Thought in New York City, Anita found her true place in the world: She pronounced the work in the Unitarian Church in Pittsburgh to be the highest fulfillment of her individual mission, leading her into the security and liberty of the Unitarian ministry. This took her to Meadville "where I found the perfect love."

Marriage and Family,
at Last

Anita Trueman spent New Year's Eve 1907 in the Beethoven Suite at Elbert Hubbard's Roycroft Inn in East Aurora, New York.[1] Just before going back to Meadville, she invoked a blessing from the new year:

I bring to the New Year better conditions and better equipment than ever before, and the promise of unfoldment is good. But one great discontent defies me. Beautiful Year, you are favorable to women. You acknowledge, with your completed square and additional day, the right of women to ask for love, for completeness in their lives. May your passing bring this great gift to me.

Before that next year, 1908, ended, Anita would marry Harold Pickett—a divinity student whom she had met on December 12, 1907, at Meadville, where she had accepted the offer of her tuition in exchange for a series of lectures on Milton's *Paradise Lost*. As their love developed, she expressed her concerns:

I have been spoiled by the affection of great men. It seems strange to think of loving a man of my own age, one who has not yet faced the battle I have been fighting these ten years. But the Infinite is behind him, and we can be sincere with each other, I believe. It would be glorious to grow on with him, and nourish the greatness in him, and sometimes to be the child I have never expressed, and rest in his love. I think

he is brave enough to leave me free in my work, and to sup-
port me in it. Help me, dear Mother, to be patient, and if
it is to be another renunciation, to be strong.

The final page in her diary of that 1907–1908 winter is in
Harold's handwriting:

The intimations of thy heart, dear soul, and the deeply
implanted yearnings for a man's love and leading, are now
in process of fulfillment. The house beautiful—our
home—is being built daily, hourly—is being framed, not by
hands, but out of the beautiful self-consecration and surren-
der of our lives to the divine process of home-making—the
eternal process to which the Divine Father-Mother calleth
us. Blessed be our Togetherness! Inspirational our daily liv-
ing! Upbuilding, our constant communion!

Anita and Harold Lionel Pickett were married on Easter Sunday
in April 1908 and spent a summer-long honeymoon tenting on the
banks of the Esopus River at her family's farm—Tremayne, in Lake
Katrine, near Kingston, New York—while awaiting Harold's first call
to a church. Their first days as husband and wife, though, were spent
at Roycroft where Anita had gone several times to lecture:

We were appointed to the very deluxe George Elliot apart-
ments the second day, but it was fitting that our marriage
should be consummated in the Beethoven Suite, where my
heart sent forth the word on New Year's Eve claiming the
love that was being prepared for me.

On April 21, she commented that the story of the past week
would match any work of fiction for romance and wonder. Harold
arrived from Meadville, very weak after a siege of "physical suffering
and terrible mental strain." She gives no explanation until the later
passages in her diary, written after their trip to Boston, but continues dramatically:

Only love for me had enabled him to come. All my devotion
was needed to lift him into life again. I gave myself to him

wholly and poured life into him. . . . My own depletion was quickly replaced with vigor by our communions. How wonderful is the love of men and women when such consecration blesses it. God's effort to know himself finds here its highest fulfillment. . . . The life that surges through the impulses of lovers arises from God's heart, reaches into Nature's and returns again. Our love is part of the cosmic romance, part of the process of creation which builds worlds.

In April 1908, watching her new husband at sleep brought forth this diary excerpt:

. . . I gazed . . . upon his beloved form lying beside me. His waking was another dawn. We thought of the day before us, the message to be given, the work to be served. Reverently and creatively, for the work's sake, we entered into that full communion of husband and wife which is the highest sacrament God has ordained. It was a sublime, perfect experience and the day justified our faith that our privilege may be used in this holy way. And if God sends children under these conditions how glorious they must be.

On May 3, they traveled to Boston to see why Harold's appointment to Norwell had been refused. She reported that they had unearthed a mystery that might have become dangerous if they had not brought it to light. At 25 Beacon Street they found all the officials vague and "inclined to scrutinize the statehouse dome while talking with us, but at last our frankness and persistence won . . . an explanation of the matter."

One of the officials, whom Anita characterized as having a big heart, took Harold aside, telling him that letters in regard to a position at Norwell had led them to suspect that there had been a reason for the sudden wedding—Anita's delicate report of this event did not mention the word *pregnant*. Because of that assumption, there was a move to get her out of their territory. All this came in connection with the Meadville faculty's withdrawal of his fellowship, so their prospects were anything but glowing when they, in all innocence, stepped into Number 25. Their frank and joyous spirit soon convinced the men of the fallacy of their assumption, but

Anita observed that letters would be necessary to correct the evidence of former ones. Anita's diary entries on this subject were incomplete and cryptic, so the specific details about the origin of the letters are missing.

May, 1908—Yesterday was the dear one's birthday and I gave him myself more fully than ever yet. He called me his birthday gift. It seems truly that I belong to no other soul in the world but him. My love has never been accepted by any other, for no one else has understood me. How many times I have passed the gate of renunciation and fought the great battle. . . . There is no other personal hold for my life in this world save Harold. God grant us many years of companionship. We are both wondrous—loved of many—but still solitary were it not for each other.

 Mother Divine, I thank thee for all gifts. . . . My Heaven is in the soul thou has given me for companion. Out of our union shall come a new earth to embody thee. We consecrate our beings to thy will. . . . God lives in us, guides and inspires us, we are learning to be artists in living.

By May 18, the newlyweds were settled into their tent on the banks of the Esopus. Anita described their idyllic existence for those first few weeks while living at River Birch Camp, the name she gave to their riverside home. "How happily I have begun the 28th year of my life in this body," she exulted. The Picketts, upon arriving in Kingston, found that her mother had prepared a lovely room for them in the old farmhouse, but they chose instead the creekside setting, where they enjoyed a pastoral existence. Their corner was wired off from the pasture where the heifers were grazing, "but the dear animals insist on being as near to us as possible." Anita said that she and Harold could hear the cows' breathing through the night "mid all the noises of these solitudes." Harold had dug out a fireplace where they cooked simple meals. "So the life of cities and institutions fade, and we dwell in eternity running a round of day and night through infinity."

Today the glory of our life found one more supreme expression. . . . Harold and I walked over to the woodlot . . .

*crossed the rye field and walked . . . along the railroad track,
carrying a box of crackers and a cake of chocolate and a copy
of Oom John's* Leaf and Tendril *just arrived. . . . On we
tramped along the open road, and plunged at last into the
wild woods. We paused at the brook which crosses the
entrance to our woodlot and drank of its cool, sweet water.
. . . The tinkle of brooks, the riotous songs of birds, the soft
rustle of leaves were the only sounds in the solitude. The
peace and purity of it all claimed us, soul and body.*

*We reverently laid aside our garments. . . . We walked
down to the little brook hand-in-hand, in the sweet innocence of children of love. How good it was to feel the free
play of my limbs and muscles and the sunshine upon my
body. Harold was glorious in the splendor of his perfect
manhood. We sat . . . upon the soft pine needles where the
sun fell freely filling us with magnetism. Then we partly
dressed and spent half-an-hour reading and another in
silence. How rich we felt as we came homeward after even
one afternoon of natural freedom. What power it will give
us for the work when we return to it. . . . In the morning
we take a plunge in the river without the formality of a
bathing suit, and we are free to go in and out of the tent
night and morning in such costume as is convenient for us.*

A delicately subtle and graceful nude photograph of Anita
always hung over the Picketts' bed, according to their daughter,
Estelle. In Anita's diary she told about the place where the photo was
taken, discovered during a walk:

*An unused path led down over steep rocks to a grotto carved
out by the waters in an angle of the stream. A wide platform
of rock, worn smooth and almost level, was intersected by
the narrow channel down which the waters rush in a steep
descent from the fairy grotto above to the one below. In the
lovely pool, we bathed and sunned our bodies in the fragrant
solitude. The grand old trees above looked down tenderly
upon the picture: two human beings living and loving in
primitive freedom. What joy such experiences are.*

Six weeks of married life had not dimmed their dream—each day led to a larger realization of its sweetness. "In our own hearts, there's a spirit of acceptance which finds the divine in all, and is determined that whatever comes shall be well, so we have met trials and joys heartily and found in each experience a way of reaching deeper unity. Each morning the awaking to our love is a new joy." And on Memorial Day, Anita noted that the social significance of this day was "another bridal" for them—that the spirit of prophecy was upon her:

I poured that love of the masses into his soul with my own. We were both glorified in this new realization of our togetherness and once more consecrated it to God. The splendor of such love surpasses all raptures of passion and we are dwelling much on the value of continence in our lives, that we build a vitality and magnetism in our bodies for the work and for our parenthood. It rejoices my soul to find Harold so ready to live this life. Thank God constantly for this great gift—my husband."

On June 2, they had to leave their pastoral home to travel to New York City, where they learned something of the conference in Boston the week before and of (Meadville) President Southworth's attitude toward their case—that the only possible course for the committee to take was to recommend another year of study for Harold to satisfy the Meadville claim of "incomplete equipment." Anita considered that to be an unjust demand, for, as she said, "they were sending out men of far inferior equipment and ability." They hoped for the situation to be modified by some action at the trustees' meeting at Meadville and prayed, "We trust all in thy keeping, Dear Father-Mother." By June 4, the Picketts were back on the Esopus, living almost entirely out-of-doors:

The moon is glorious this first quarter and we have moved our couch out on the bank where we can watch it set beyond the hills across the creek. This evening we are writing and reading with our lamp and table out under the sky. A glorious mellow sunset melted into twilight before our letters and reading were more than begun, so we are having this unique experience. The bright moon seems to glimmer but faintly at the zenith and the darkness about seems even more dense than when one steps out into the night from a brilliantly lighted room.

But if Anita and Harold were not concerned about their future, her parents were. Anita revealed that a recent letter from her father was a painful experience, with its expressed worry from both Truemans about the uncertainty of the young couple's plans. She loyally pronounced that Harold was noble about this series of prodding letters, declaring that they were determined to live their happy life together and win their way into the hearts of others. "We know that we have done all in our power and that each effort will bear fruit." On June 21, once more waxing eloquent about her love, she wrote that in those days Harold was the "occasion and object" of her whole life, and the

. . . repository of my thoughts. We are building the beauty of our environment, the blessing of companionship, which has come into our life, and the vigor and satisfaction of our work into our souls. Going over the old journals, I mark a contrast between the life of solitude and renunciation, and my present life of intimate companionship and rich consecration. Both are good in season and no life is well-rounded without periods of both. The great joy is in having known the wonders of solitude and carrying their significance into a life of active service. There are moments and moods of meditation in these days which serve to bring our souls into closer communion through sharing the divine mystery that underlies all expression.

And on July 19, she spoke for the first time of planning for a child, saying "surely the time is auspicious. After more than a week of conjugal separation, we were ready to give rich vitality to the holy sacrament of procreation":

Glorious music and beauty in myriad forms have been the accompaniment of our work in these precious days. I have been writing a poem, too, and preparing for next season's

lecture work, so the child, if he is with us, is launched for service in the world, and for joy and beauty and love. . . . he should come when the Easter moon is full to bless the first anniversary of our wedding.

By August 8, she began to speak more confidently about the coming of a child:

My glorious husband has been wondrously tender and strong in the trial. Each problem of our married life brings some new glory of his soul into expression. I thank thee, dear Mother, for him and I thank thee for the promise of motherhood which now seems assured. It is sweet to lie here and dream of it and I pray thee, beloved, to protect the little one from any danger. . . . I want to give my husband a healthy, joyous child. Nature knows. Trust her.

An echo of the unconventional Anita—she who would have dared to have a child out of wedlock—is in the diary passage reporting that the marriage certificate seemed in danger of being lost, as it meant so little to them in itself, "so I place it here as one of the mementoes of this memorable year. Our marriage was truly wrought in the heart of God, and is part of the cosmic romance, needing no outward signs."

In September, while waiting in Boston to hear if there would be any work, they were down to their last $1.29. Shortly after they retired to bed, the bell rang and a drayman appeared with their box of books from Lake Katrine. They had been hoping it would be delayed a few days, after the custom of freight shipments, that they might be better prepared to meet the expense. It proved to be only about half what they expected, however—$1.26—leaving them with three cents still in the treasury.

They slept in confidence that the next step would be provided for and rose with curiosity to meet the day that must open the way for it. While Anita prepared breakfast, Harold unpacked the books and the study took on a homelier air than before as the familiar volumes found their places on the shelves. Suddenly with a shout of delight, he bounded into the kitchen; he had remembered two lucky pennies that he had carried for years. These were stacked with the other three to make up carfare to carry him to Boston, where he hoped to find an appointment for preaching the next day—and to secure payment in advance. They joked a little about it, questioning whether it would be worthwhile for him to walk to Boston and save the pennies.

The doorbell rang. There stood a friend and colleague, Bertland Morrison. The Picketts knew then that they were saved. Morrison advanced them a dollar, enabling Anita to buy ice and some necessary groceries. The peddler trusted her for eggs and vegetables, so she was able to serve a good dinner and lay in a fine stock of food. The two men went down to Number 25 to get their appointments, returning at noon with eager appetites and happy hearts: Harold was flourishing a $10 bill, about half of which would go for train fare to Northfield, where he would preach. Anita wrote, "[B]etter openings will come later. But this is a brave beginning." On October 6, 1908, her ecstatic diary entry left no doubt as to her impending motherhood:

> *My soul doth magnify the Lord. How few women in all history have been so richly blessed as I. Six months of marital happiness are almost past. For three precious months the great mystery of motherhood has been with me.*

During her pregnancy, she expressed her views, presumably shared by Harold, about sexuality and its role in their lives, that the "mere naturalness" regarding sexual relations as simply a means of the periodical relief of physical stress, and, incidentally or primarily, as the means of procreation, was not sufficient for them. She proclaimed that the relation between a man and a woman as united as they, was sexual throughout and that

> *. . . the more of our love flows into our work, the less strain there is on our physical relation. There has been no strain between us, thank God, but only a need for adjustment arising from outside influences. We are ardent lovers, and our love is all joy. Through the day, while we are at work, every smile and word and touch of our affection is an inspiration. The life force flows creatively through us. There is no local stimulus except in the occasional love-feast after the day's*

work is done and we are resting together. I am more and more convinced that at any rate during my pregnancy it will be best for us to sleep in separate beds, and so have moved Harold's couch into my room so that he may be near me, but not so near that our magnetism will be aroused to a point that needs control. When we are settled in our own house, I shall surely arrange the twin beds which seem to me the ideal furnishing of the marital chamber.

On October 22, their landlady demanded that the furniture be returned, leaving them with few furnishings in their apartment. As was typical for Anita, she turned it into a positive event, saying that those days had been rich in spiritual experience—"to know how little material things mean is to have wealth which possessions cannot bestow. Our love, the only abiding thing in this life, has revealed new depths. Divine Mother, I will not cling to this best of all thy gifts, but I can let all else slip away if this remains, and without it, all else would be empty."

In the midst of a meeting during her pregnancy, she mused over her child, saying that she could not help thinking of her baby, safely cradled under her heart and sharing this vital experience. And afterward, when she went back to Harold, who whispered, "You wonderful woman," Anita could feel the baby's life throbbing in response to the applause. "There's a prophecy of your own life, I hope, in such an occasion." Anita proudly recorded that people were saying that she was a great demonstration to the womenfolk. Several present that morning were astounded when informed of her condition. She thanked God if she might be the means of eliminating some of the fear of pregnancy and foolishness of feminine fashions. She trusted that the confinement would be a great demonstration of the value of a spiritual attitude and natural methods. She said, "I do not shrink from suffering. Motherhood is worth all the possible cost."

The Cosmic
Marriage Falters

One of the first times Anita noted that all was not idyllic in the Pickett marriage was on November 2, 1908, when she cited an example of the conflict between her own mystical approach and Harold's practical approach to life and to philosophy. This was an ongoing cry in her diaries throughout her life—disappointment that they were not kindred souls in their thinking, as she had hoped and, at first, thought:

> After the lecture Thursday evening, we had one of our fruit-less philosophical discussions. Harold said some harsh things of my work and my message, which made me feel the tragic loneliness of my inner life. I broke down under it and, for a few moments, a fit of hysterical grief possessed me and I shut out the light of my life: his love. It was a terrible experience for both of us. Our first thought was for the child. I strove to check my passion and Harold to comfort me, and he came leagues nearer to my soul in the agony of it all.

Harold admitted to Anita that a temperamental prejudice against the esoteric aspect of life prevented his sharing her deepest consciousness. He wanted to get everything into the terms of philo-sophical argument or practical expression. To enjoy the inner life for its own sake seemed to him futile; to acknowledge that there are ranges of life open to one which cannot be translated into words or action hurt "the intellectual pride of the philosopher." He imagined that to care at all for these things robbed the outer life of some of the sanctity that he poured into it so richly.

Anita wrote, "[A]nd how I have fought against it. But it need not and must not be so. There is a life transcending senses and reason which continues after the senses and intellect of this life fall to decay, and it is worthwhile to cultivate that eternal life now." She continued, saying that it cannot be explained by one knowing it to one not knowing it. In Harold's case she was assured that he did know it in large measure, but willfully shut it off. "At times we almost enter the sanctuary together and I know the time will come when we shall share this best of all blessings."

She went on to say that she must learn, in the meantime, to be content to live that part of life alone, and to justify her faith in it by living more richly and calmly in the outer life. She cautioned that she must not get excited or hurried over her work, or allow herself to care so intensely about the little differences of opinion that seemed to "cloud the bright morning of our love. Harold, let us grow together."

Although there is little evidence that Anita's lecture circuit continued at its previous pace, there remains a list of lectures that were available in 1908 and 1909:

The Test of Wisdom
The Psychology of Success
The Psychology of Happiness
Sensitiveness and Strength
The Problem of Good and Evil
The Relation of Labor and Art
Philosophy of Work
The Philosophy of Freedom
Psychology of Character
The Philosophy of Friendship
The Problem of Personal Duty
The Psychology of Mental Healing
Henry George: The Prophet of Social Freedom
Walt Whitman: The Prophet of Spiritual Freedom
The Roycrofters and Their Work

Her promotional literature stated that, in addition to the above special lectures, she was prepared to give courses of six lectures each on the following themes:

The Evolution of Individuality

The Path to Realization

The Inner Meaning of Milton's *Paradise Lost*

The Teachings of Krishna and the *Baghavad Gita*

Additionally, the flyer stated that for terms, dates, and other information, address Harold L. Pickett, Roycroft Inn, East Aurora, Erie County, New York.

On March 3, 1909, as they approached the celebration of their first year of marriage, she observed in her diary:

> *A year ago today, Harold and I were in Franklin [Pennsylvania] together, meeting the supreme test of our love and our faith in each other. How terrible was that wild tramp among the oil derricks on the hill overlooking Franklin, when the world threatened to come between us, yet in the darkest moments of those hours of agony, I verily believe we had faith in each other and in the destiny of our love. What strength God wrought in our souls in that tragic afternoon and what supreme joy was granted in the holy night that followed.*
>
> *That was our real marriage—from henceforth we were one, in a union which the state might ratify and the church consecrate, but which no human institution could influence. From that hour we have grown together as one life—in our work, our purpose.*

The assumption is that Harold was not going to graduate, thus jeopardizing their chance to marry and be together. Since the previous chapter marks the shift from her autobiography to her diaries alone, we are missing some of her expositions, and therefore must sometimes draw our own conclusions.

The young couple began their life-long ministries to Unitarian congregations with Harold's settlement at Sandwich, Massachusetts, in 1909, followed soon after by a stint in Boise, Idaho. Anita's presence was always a strong one in Harold's pastorates—these first two and, later, the East Lexington, Hudson, Peabody, and Woburn (Massachusetts) churches. While in Boise, she cast her first vote and said that, in Idaho, women had all the privileges of citizenship and the responsibilities. Voting was indeed a great experience for Anita, and she expressed the hope it would not be long before the citizens of Massachusetts would enact an equal suffrage law, so that women there might have the right to take their true place in public affairs.

Also in Boise came their first serious marital difficulty. Although most of the pages to those diaries were destroyed, there are enough passages left to piece together a partial story. In her last years, Estelle, their firstborn daughter, spoke of her father's having succumbed to the prevailing Mormon belief in multiple marriages, then widely held in Boise, and having proposed taking a second wife. Whatever ensued, we know that he left Anita with a new baby, Trueman, born in 1911, and must have taken the two-year-old Estelle with him, since Anita later spoke of their daughter having

Anita, Trueman (later John), Estelle, and Harold

convinced him to come back. Anita wrote in her 1913 diary, right after the birth of their third child Laurel:

> *Trueman is two years old today. He is such a splendid big boy and Daddy is quite infatuated with him. How thankful I am that we are all together. A year ago, Trueman and I were snowbound on the prairies of Western Kansas [en route to Columbus, Ohio, Harold's parents' home]. God grant we may never be divided again. Yet I thank God that by that cruel separation we were led to a holier union than we had formerly dreamed of.*

On Easter Sunday, Anita observed that it was a year today since she and Trueman had joined Harold in Columbus—that one by one the echoes of their last year's tragedy were dying as the anniversaries passed, leaving her the wonderful new realization of the blessings that the terrible experience failed to destroy. She wrote, "[T]he old deep realities arise touched with new glory, having passed through the purifying flames. Thank God for it all."

The most telling diary entry came years later, right after Harold's death in 1950, when she enclosed a little notice that there was a Unitarian Fellowship being organized in Boise, Idaho, and wrote:

> *So—Boise is waking up again, dear. What a hard time we had there. When you left me there to go east and get a divorce, it was a more cruel separation than death, but how wonderful was the sequel—how our little daughter turned your heart back to me, and how the girl who wanted you so madly renounced her passion and set you free. It killed the Unitarian Church in Boise, but now after nearly forty years, it is reviving. Your true spirit will be in this new work there. It was the effect of living in Mormon surroundings—a curious warped idealism about the glory of sacrifice in love we lived through. It was, indeed, far more bitter while it lasted than this complete separation.*

There did seem to be a black cloud following Harold's ministry throughout his lifetime. Veiled references in the diaries and comments from their daughter, Estelle, indicate that he was dismissed from other churches for involvement with women. He was very handsome and was admired by women, and, in Estelle's words, "sometimes it just lapped over." It is obvious to the reader of Anita's many diaries and her autobiography that she did forgive Harold his transgressions and continued to love him dearly throughout their lifetime together. Her diaries were her sounding board for disappointments and frustrations. Still she always followed those complaints with positive comments that his being such a glorious lover made it all worthwhile!

Little survived of the diaries from the Boise years, but newspaper clippings indicate that Anita's early fame followed her there and may have somewhat stolen the limelight from Harold. The headlines screamed:

REMARKABLE AND FAMOUS WOMAN HAS COME TO BOISE TO MAKE HOME

CAREER OF MRS. PICKETT ONE OF GREAT INTEREST—LECTURES AND WRITINGS OF WIFE OF PASTOR OF UNITY CHURCH HAVE ATTRACTED WIDE ATTENTION

"WAGES OF SIN" IS WOMAN'S THEME—MRS. ANITA TRUEMAN PICKETT DELIVERS NOTABLE SERMON AT UNITY CHURCH

FOUND INSPIRATION IN HENRY GEORGE—WELL KNOWN LECTURER MAKES HOME HERE

MRS. ANITA TRUEMAN PICKETT, NOTED LECTURER, TALKS OF EAST AURORA

FOUR LECTURES BY MRS. PICKETT ON MILTON'S POEM, *PARADISE LOST* THE BASIS FOR AN INTELLECTUAL TREAT FOR BOISE STUDENTS

TELLS OF GOOD AND EVIL—MRS. PICKETT DRAWS LESSONS FROM *PARADISE LOST*

WIFE OF UNITARIAN PASTOR ARRIVES; IS A NOTED LECTURER—Mrs. Anita Trueman Pickett, one of the most prominent woman lecturers in the eastern states, and wife of Rev. Pickett, who recently accepted a call to become pastor of the Unitarian church here, arrived this morning to join her husband and will in the future make her home in this city. For the last six weeks she has been giving a course of lectures in eastern cities.

One of these articles stated that she had filled more than two thousand lecture engagements in the ten years of her public work, a statistic not found elsewhere in her diaries or autobiographies.

Anita noted in her diary that during their time in Boise, Idaho, there was a very low church budget, so Harold had to work somewhere else—on the Maysonholder Ranch, Owyhee County, Idaho. There is a receipt from Messers Arch Maysonholder and Isaac Johnson for the sum of $35 in cash and $100 worth of Owyhee Ozone and Medical Treatments, as payment in full for three weeks' work in haying on a ranch in Jackson Creek, Idaho.

In spite of Anita's fame, when President Taft (a Unitarian) visited Boise, Harold—as minister of Unity Church—was invited to ride in a motorcade and attend a reception for him, with no mention of Anita being invited. This was the first recorded instance of the discounting of her contribution as acting cominister of the churches Harold served. There would be many more, even in churches where she officially coministered.

Since Anita spoke spontaneously, with only written notes, few of her sermons have survived, but one entitled "Knowledge and Faith" was published in the Boise, Idaho, newspaper during her time spent there. It may be found in the Readings at the end of this book.

In 1913, while awaiting the birth of Laurel, their third child, in East Lexington, Massachusetts, she wrote that she had never felt so close to God as in some recent hours of resting in Harold's arms, with the "full sweetness of my motherhood quietly transfusing all my being":

Thank God for it all, and God grant me patience and strength as the days bring their burdens and their problems as well as their joys. Thank God for this little home: the temple of love and service. May no cloud darken it. I have strange presentiments of sorrow to be met. Perhaps it is only the "pillar of cloud by day," the sense of the world's sorrow which the soul can not forget. Let me never forget, dear Mother, and when the night darkens over my own path, keep thy pillar of fire before me. Never in hours of deepest sorrow and shame has that light deserted me. I'm assured that every step of the way is thine. I follow.

After Laurel's birth In 1913, Anita was feeling a special kind of peace and joy in the family that inspired her to write:

Firelight from our own hearth, moonlight over our own garden, three lovely babies bathed and put to bed, our sweetpeas planted to celebrate the fifth anniversary of our marriage: so we enter upon another year, and tomorrow we shall both preach as we did our first Sunday.

An excerpt from Harold's diary from 1913 related a charming incident concerning Trueman, then two years and two months old, who escaped from his caretaker at church and came calmly up the pulpit steps to a seat between his father and mother during the voluntary and "there he sat with his sober blue eyes of glory and halo of golden hair, until I took him down into a pew during the sermon by his mother. He listened a quarter hour very still, then fell asleep in my arms with his big yellow shock on my shoulder."

Another entry, written on their fifth anniversary, confirmed his pride and joy in his marriage and family:

Our 5th wedding anniversary—a big cake to celebrate it. Our happiest days seem to be the newest ones. God has blessed us more than thought can know, or tongue express—Estelle, Trueman, Laurel—these three dear sweet blessings name our riches and token [sic] our joys.

Finally—Ordination
to Unitarian Ministry

From the time of Anita's marriage to Harold Pickett in 1908 until her ordination to the ministry in 1921, she preached a total of seventy-five times at Unitarian churches, including a 4 P.M. sermon in Garrettsville, Ohio, after their 10 A.M. wedding on April 19, 1908. This was in addition to giving many lectures and teaching religious education, as well as helping her husband in his ministerial duties. In one of Harold's diaries, he wrote:

> [The] Parish meeting of Follen Church voted to call me. The young people of the church held an informal meeting some days before and urged immediate action on the part of the church because they had heard Mrs. Pickett speak recently and had fallen in love with her and wanted her to come here to live and work.

In 1913, while Harold served as minister of the Follen Church in East Lexington, Massachusetts, Anita reflected on the stresses of playing these several roles. Laurel, her third child in four years, was nine months old when Anita wrote in her diary:

> *In old days women like me would have been branded "common scold" and forced to wear some badge of public contempt. I despise myself utterly for I have lost my temper several times with the children this morning and I must admit that the condition of hysteria that I am fighting is*

more the effect than the cause of these outbursts. God strengthen me and grant me patience.

Another diary entry notes that Anita was thinking of sending Estelle back with Aunt Annie to stay with Mother Pickett in Ohio. She told of losing patience when she tried to teach Estelle a word in one of her books "and her complete stupidity about it frightened and angered me. We wore each other out about it and I am convinced she is not yet ready for any sustained mental effort, so she had better go to her grandma and have a good time this winter." Anita admitted that she really needed relief from the presence of caring for all three, though she could hardly bear to think of missing any more time out of Estelle's life. "She is growing dearer to me every day. I must remember to give her sweet memories to keep these days," Anita wrote.

On January 22, 1914, she wrote of having learned the hard way that she must focus totally on the work in order for it to be successful. Her talk for the Alliance in Lexington the week before had been a great disappointment to her, but she learned some valuable lessons from the experience—that if she were to do this work, she must treat it as earnestly "as of old. . . . It is no casual matter to bear the very gift of life and it needs preparation of mind and soul. It is not one of many things, it is the great central thing." She wrote that she had been sewing and conversing until the meeting was called to order; then, instead of going out for a while during the business meeting, she stayed and let her mind follow it all. When the lecture began, both she and the audience were mentally tired. In further conjecture on what went wrong, she said that she might have asked them to adjourn to the adjoining hall, but they were sewing for the district nurse and she did not want to ask them to give her their whole attention. Thus they sat about at all angles, and "I talked but with more confusion than conviction." So to prepare for the lecture series at Emerson Hall, she begged off from an all-day Alliance meeting and a dentist appointment to stay at home with Laurel and "seek true inspiration."

Surely the spirit of [Ralph Waldo] Emerson, whose ministry was in the same hall, might be invoked. The atmosphere of his presence has not been cultivated since his departure.

These lectures will come nearer to his mission than any to which the hall has been put these many years. So dear Big Brother Soul, Immortal Comrade, pour the intention of thy message into my words. . . . Charles Wesley Emerson, my noble friend and teacher in this life reach to thy immortal soul for the strength of oratory to stir the hearts of these people. "The immediate environment of every soul is spiritual."

On February 1, 1914, Anita wrote of attending a great lecture on "Woman and the State" in Lexington Town Hall. She said that she gave a word of testimony as a "disenfranchised citizen and it covered a point not considered in the lecture." On February 19, Anita wrote of the monotony of life day after day with the little ones in most unsatisfactory housing, without water and drainage. She said that the solitude of that snowbound retreat would be fruitful of thought if her mind were not chained to continual small services for "my little king and queen and the dear lord of this home." (During this time, Estelle had been with her grandmother Pickett for six months.)

When Anita was to give the second of her lectures in Emerson Hall, she commented that she felt about as intelligent as a "setting hen," and that the next day she would go to Billerica for an Alliance lecture, feeling as if she had nothing to give. In her constant attempts to improve and perfect her performance, and to do battle with the devils of dissatisfaction and frustration, she made this list:

Here then are some rules to be observed in these coming days with the help of God and all angels.

1—Early rising, solitude, meditation

2—Health, deep breathing, out-of-doors

3—Self-control, calmness, cheerfulness, silence

4—Deal with people spiritually, especially the children "You cannot help others while they can hinder you."

5—Give every moment possible to literary work

6—Obedience in external matters, have no will, shape all things from within.

God help me in this task of self-mastery. How rebellious the lower self is. . . . Even where my love is greatest, a perversity which seems beyond government prevents my expressing it. Sometimes I wonder that my husband can love me as he does, and I do not wonder at the trouble I have with the children, for they are living mirrors of myself. Thank God I can see how vile and miserable I am. O, patient spirit of Christ, enter my heart and free me from bondage to self. Take my bodily strength and use it in the daily service to the home. All that I am I dedicate to God. Of myself I am helpless. Be thou my help.

By December 13, 1914, Anita must have received some unexpected invitations to preach, for her diary chronicled her joy in the widening of their work. She observed that the extra money earned went partly to pay for some household help, her new glasses, Christmas gifts, and a Christmas party for the children. She thanked God for the opportunity of such service, saying it was life to her; that she would be glad to preach every Sunday. "I get so discouraged and tired when I do nothing but housework," she wrote.

And on that New Year's Eve, Anita counted her blessings, chiding herself for wanting more. Her prayer to God was that they might enter upon the new year with their comfortable house and three lovely children, their health, and their rich opportunities:

I consecrate all this and pray that the true spirit of faith may possess us. Surely if we do well the work which lies before us each day, we need not be ambitious for greater accomplishment. If we use well the gifts each day brings, we need not suffer the sting of desire. A steady purpose, a serene hope: may these give force and enthusiasm to our lives. The world will have need of strong sober sweet souls.

One can only imagine how much criticism she incurred for leading a dual life, at a time when women were encouraged to stay home. Her diary recorded one such episode concerning one of the other ministers' wives, whose mood of criticism turned on Anita for wanting to intersperse her domestic life with an occasional dip into the larger life. Just as Anita was leaving her, she began, "as an older woman," to advise Anita to give all her time and thought to her family:

What she meant to say I did not have time to learn but her introduction was in words which have given my faith a new strength: "No one can serve two masters." I have one master—even God. How often in the old days I returned to this, when confused by human advice and criticism. I have one master and so it is today. My master gives me my tasks and my strength. With the trust of a child, with the loyalty of a faithful servant, may I follow it.

I'm assured in my heart that my voice is to serve the gospel of truth and freedom—whether now or in later days matters not. Only be aware of ambition and vanity, my soul. Do thy day's work, caring for the house and children is part of it, and when the need for the word calls thee to wider fields, the help at home will be provided. Surely the first duty is to make the children and their father happy. This I could do much better if I could do more preaching and less housework. But that must be decided by the divine law. In all events, I must keep the home happy.

On March 5 she wrote that she had to give a lecture on the disenfranchised woman for the Suffrage League and also one on economy and wealth for the Alliance. A passage in her 1915 diary showed that, in her understanding of her role as a wife, she was subject to much of society's influence. The dichotomy found in these diary passages seems to be a way she worked through her resentments against the constriction of the times. After nearly every complaint, she scolded and reminded herself of positive aspects of home and family. In considering a move, she wrote that Harold would have his work, but she would have to cultivate graces rather foreign to her and give up work that was dear to her, adding that "it's the man's place to say the word, the wife's to up and follow," and that she could find beauty and happiness anywhere. She expressed that the children were her chief interest in life for a few years—that the new place would be good for them.

Meanwhile Harold's star was rising somewhat. In 1914, he received the $40 Billings Prize from Harvard Divinity School, where he was taking some courses, for improvement in "pulpit delivery." It was signed by Henry Wilder Foot, secretary of the faculty. And in 1915, while attending Tufts College, he won a $40 prize, the annual Goddard's Prize Readings, with "Alfred Noyes: Rank and File." Anita's diaries reflected only pride in her husband and no jealousy of his accomplishments.

While at the East Lexington Church, Anita first mentioned the Reverend William Channing Gannett, mentor and inspirational force for feminist minister Antoinette Brown Blackwell.[1] Anita reported that their little church had entertained this poet preacher, whose words were sung over all the world and who had been the minister of that church forty-three years ago. She told how a wonderful reverence filled the place as the venerable saintly face beamed upon them in a long moment of silence before the rich voice (unspoiled by his deafness) began to pour forth a stream of reminiscences and exhortations. They sang several of his hymns, and the children of his old parishioners greeted him in the name of those departed. The spell of his benediction was wonderful—sweetly spiritual yet tenderly human. "He has an aptitude for spontaneous poetic expression which is charming," Anita proclaimed. A few years later, she quoted from a letter he wrote from Rochester, New York, where he was celebrating his eightieth birthday: "Happy the two where the parsoness so supplements the parson."

Although Anita's diary keeping was largely confined to personal commentary, there were occasional references to the wider world. One such passage, in 1917, referred to Jeannette Rankin, born one year before Anita. Montana Congresswoman Rankin had voted her conscience, unpopular though her vote was, when she answered the roll call with "I want to stand by my country, but I cannot vote for war. I vote no!" As she did so, she thought of the promise she had made to the Montana voters: "I will do everything in my power to keep our country out of war and your sons safe at home," and it gave her the courage to cast an "unpatriotic" vote. Anita wrote:

We are at war. The House voted early this morning in favor of the resolution—Jeannette Rankin, the first woman in

Congress, being among the fifty who voted against it. I'm glad she was true to her womanhood.

In 1920, the last year before Anita was ordained a minister in the Unitarian Church, she drafted a manuscript titled "My Religion." It follows:

After passing through an orthodox conversion in childhood, and reclaiming spiritual elimination in early youth, after preaching the truth then revealed in me for 24 years, after listening to professors of theology and reading the works of philosophers, after many conflicts with self and bearing my part in the World War still being waged, after wrestling with the problems of motherhood for a dozen years, I came to a certain hilltop crowned with pines and maples and birches where I held communion with God, reviewing the past and projecting the future. What, after all this experience, I asked, is my religion, that I may teach it in simple words to my children and preach it to my people, that I might test my own thought, direct my action, and cast my ballot for truth.

The Spirit answered, "It is even that which was given thee in the beginning: To realize and reveal the divine within thee, and to see, serve and worship the divine in all else. This is religion; it is abundance of life; it is art, philosophy, science. It is history, progress, civilization, destiny. It is God realizing his own being more fully in thy consciousness. It is God creating the Kingdom of Heaven. It is God beholding this Universe through revealing His beauty to thee.

"This is love, one nature in the cohesion of matter, gravitations of worlds, the affinities of forces, the attractions of friendship, the passion of sex, the aspiration which reunites the soul with its source. It is the self divided into many selves that in each it may enfold a beholder and revealer of its being, reaching out eagerly to all other beholders and revealers. So infinitely multiplying its infinite life. To know this exalts all human experience of love beyond any dream."

Anita expounded on the Unitarianism she perceived in 1920, commenting that the "first person singular was the new thought emphasis," thus making the content of religion available to each soul, instead of leaving broad generalizations and abstract theories up in the air. She suggested that this change of emphasis was what was needed to make Unitarianism dynamic.

Harold was settled in the Peabody, Massachusetts, church by 1920. In her journal written then, she spoke of ministers being changed around and of how these changes were of interest to the pulpit supply committee, and, as the Picketts marched on to the half-century mark, of interest to them. She wrote that unless they were "hopelessly mediocre (which may be true) we ought to find a place in one of the larger churches within a few years or else some larger field of official service. So speaks ambition, yet faithful service in the several fields we now reach has its value, though it promises so little for the future. "

She insisted that it was more precious to share with her husband the faith that God would lead them and that the way would be opened for their feet, than it was to win success and promotion on any other ground than real service. Nevertheless, with the passing of years, Anita wondered if they were making the most of them. "How much time," she asked, "have we lost through mistakes and offences?" She wrote that, indeed, they had been fortunate not to lose more, and they had grown spiritually through all the experiences of their unusual careers: "So we will trust the soul of life and go on in the appointed paths."

The appointed path finally led Anita to her true place as an ordained Unitarian minister, when the call came from the Rowe, Massachusetts, church to be its summer minister—a post she held from 1921 to 1926. Her ordination was based on her life experiences as a preacher of Free Thought philosophy as well as her years of helping her husband in his pastorates. A newspaper reporter from Woburn, Massachusetts, where Harold had assumed yet another ministry, reported on her ordination:

An unusual ceremony, never before performed in Woburn and rarely if ever experienced in the annals of the Unitarian church will be solemnized here Sunday night when Mrs. Anita Trueman Pickett, wife of the pastor of the Unitarian church, will be ordained in her husband's church and by a woman clergyman . . . with her husband as one of the officiating clergymen. . . . Rev. Florence Buck, D.D., a woman connected with the AUA headquarters in Boston, will conduct the ordination ceremonies. Ordination could have been conferred on Mrs. Pickett at any time, her qualifications having been sufficient to entitle her to admittance to the list of the clergy. . . . The ordination of a woman is a ceremony rarely witnessed and there has never been a case in the knowledge of Woburn Unitarians where the wife of the pastor had ever been ordained in the church of which her husband was pastor and at which he participated.

Later, while being considered for the Barnard Memorial Church in Boston, she met with a Mr. Cornish, who told her that there were some meddlesome people there who might give her trouble, but that she could probably dispel or evade that difficulty. He said, "Bless you, Mrs. Pickett, you can do lots of things that other people can't. Go ahead!"

The winters saw her filling the pulpit at Barnard Memorial Church; although she referred to her title as "superintendent rather than minister," in newspaper articles of the time she was listed as the pastor. In a diary passage she expressed concern over whether she would be able to handle that placement in addition to her family obligations: "A larger question is whether a minister has any room for criticism and impatience in her consciousness."

At Hingham, Massachusetts, when she told a friend and colleague, Houghton Page, of her new task as superintendent, he said: "It will be a success if you have anything to do with it." She wrote: "I set these words in my heart for power when trials come." The trials soon came. It indeed became a situation demanding more than she could give, in so short a time, with greater wisdom than she felt she yet possessed. In 1921 she wrote that the ordeal was over, that "I'm conscious that I must have seemed a flagrant egotist. This, however, put me on the level with the man who did not hesitate to criticize and challenge my position."

She had been speaking out to plead for more personal service on the part of the minister, more concrete understanding of people's spiritual problems. telling about the work being done by many self-appointed, but consecrated, spiritual helpers outside the church, and urging that such a help should be given by ministers. At one such talk, Dr. Sam Eliot, who left as soon as she ceased speaking, objected to her line of thought almost completely as favoring introspection and self-centered thinking. She felt that she had failed utterly to get her message over to him. Anita stated that he warned the ministers against placing too much emphasis on personal ministry, saying his cure-all was to give people something to do for the church. "There spoke the president of the AUA, who for more than 20 years has been detached from the parish ministry, which deals directly with average busy people. How many problems need the very opposite treatment for solution?" she asked.

In March 1922, her diary noted that she gave a talk on personal spiritual discipline. She spoke on various types of religion: Evangelism, Orthodoxy, Fundamentalism, Christian Science and its derivatives, and Theosophy, elaborating on what effect the theory of each one has on personal character:

Should that the Unitarian church aims at collective service, leaving character to develop naturally, while the redemptive religions aim first at salvation, trusting the soul to overflow in service, chiefly of the missionary type. We have not given sufficient attention to personal training and healing, so we have failed to draw many who should belong to us.

The talk seemed to be appreciated, though it was hard at first for her to secure the attention of the audience. Anita was disappointed in the occasion—she said that she could have made so much more of the subject, yet perhaps she gave all they could assimilate and, on another occasion, would plan to develop the material in better form.

While a guest speaker at Cohasset, Massachusetts, she described the quaint old meeting house with its high pulpit and its choir in a side gallery, saying that going from the minister's room at the rear of the gallery, down the stairs, up the aisle, and up the steep pulpit stairs made quite a processional for her. She buttoned herself into the pretty upholstered box with its two crimson brocade panels behind, its crimson velvet lectern, and its great leather-bound Bible in front and "never felt more at home in my life. . . . I think the fee of $25 was the largest I ever earned on a single occasion except the $40 or more which was given to me on the occasion of my lecture at Dr. Egbert Guernsey's in New York 22 years ago!"

While guest preaching at Kennebunk, Maine, she observed that she was to carry the word of life and immortality to the people of that parish. "Not a new word, but O, Mother Divine, make it fresh and liveable to these dear people." For a series of Sunday afternoon addresses at the First Parish Church in Dorcester, Massachusetts, Anita preached on New Thought, as perceived in 1922. A review reads, "Mrs. Pickett is well-known in New Thought Circles and has brought the best of their thinking with her into the Unitarian Ministry."

During this same period, while Anita was lecturing at Emerson College on extemporaneous speech, she stopped to visit in the Metaphysical Club. She said, "It led an old Unitarian back toward her spiritual home." Also in 1922, she reported that Fundamentalism was the great issue then, and that it had been challenged in three successive issues of *The Christian Register*. She wrote that the *Boston Herald* had taken it up and the mailbag was full of the controversy. "Our people need instruction and counsel. I'm thankful that I can contribute a little."

Always Anita's thoughts came back to her family and its struggles—one time over an attempt to get the family to systematize its housekeeping. She said that her own will assumed a dictatorial manner when she was trying to demand cooperation—and then all was lost. Harold would countermand her orders to the children; they would then play their parents off against each other. She wrote, "[W]e are a centrifugal family anyway, and it is going to call for deep devotion to hold us in harmony while we occupy the same house . . . then, too, other people and their idiosyncrasies intrude upon our peace so long as I am all ambition for the work of the church. God, give me light and strength each day to see what is my duty and do it."

Anita's feminism, although mild for our times, prompted her to deplore the idea among New Englanders that it is a virtue for a woman to sacrifice herself for her family, especially her parents. "She naturally feels then that she owns them, that she has bought them with the blood of sacrifice, and if they show any desire for freedom, she clutches them mercilessly."

In July 1922, while exploring options for her uncertain future, Anita mused over whether they would be at the Rowe Church for another summer or not. A friend urged her to go in for Chatauqua work. She had been thinking that her family might rig up a caravan and cover the circuit in it while she lectured on the American home and the American family, motherhood and the state, and kindred subjects. She stated that she would like to travel widely and study home and family life in other countries, in order to gather material for her lectures.

Anita had read a book on freedom that inspired her to comment that she, too, had secured her freedom with a price; the book was something of a help to her in its exaggeration of the dangers confronting any woman who tries to be anything other than the conventional wife and mother:

> *How natural it is for these domestic interests to claim all a woman's true strength and attention. I cannot claim a few minutes of retirement without interruption, especially in these summer days, with the children and their friends about all the while.*
>
> *Harold has been here a whole week and that means days broken up by his irregular habits, and his eagerness to take me on little trips. It means nights that are not restful because they are so sweet with his presence. When he goes away, I cannot always profit by solitude, for Laurel wants to sleep with me. Harold has a nagging way of interfering with my housekeeping, but Estelle helps a lot with the work, and Trueman and Laurel do most of the errands.*

While at Rowe, Massachusetts, in the summer of 1923, her diary again recorded her agony over the difficulties of raising a family, while also pursuing her life's work: She wrote that surely it would seem that she spent her life fully with her family, but when she begged for an hour of quiet or to be spared the string of inconsequent questions, which seem to be saved up for Sunday morning, they made her feel that she was abusing them by being a minister, "though it is my professional work which secures them this summer home." She continued, saying that sometimes the problems of family life would grow acute, leaving her feeling inadequate to the personal task and unworthy of the larger calling. "We've had a desperate struggle with impudence and impishness in Trueman and only a severe punishment seemed able to break the spell. Since then he's been angelic. It is shameful that we cannot correct him except by force. It was a bitter experience and clouded several days with its shadow." Anita commented that Estelle was "her strength and stay and my constant delight. She is so calm and clear-minded, appreciative and generous. She gives me faith that Trueman, too, will get beyond the Penrod stage before long."

Trueman had lately made new claims upon her motherhood. "I hardly know you, even as a friend," he said to her one day quite passionately. When she asked him to explain his inarticulate protest against her work, he admitted that she did as much for him as other mothers did, spent as much time with her children, and took them with her in most of her work, but he revealed that he was jealous of her public. "I want a mother that is mine and not always somebody else's. I hardly know you, even as a friend." he said. Anita wrote that she guessed that she had been away from the house too much:

> *Then we had a good talk which drew us very close together. He has been so careless and disrespectful in his attitude toward me, I never dreamed he had any sentimental regard for me, but he insisted that he wants to stay here and go to high school so's to be at home, and I have promised to spend an hour each evening with him as far as possible. This home life is the thing to be cherished for the children. Harold and I would be contented Nomads. Camping, traveling and hotel life would suit us if we had our work to live for, but the children must have happy memories of home. How I hunger sometimes for the chance to live the full professional life, to organize my time in the service of the work I can do well. My desk, in the course of our thoroughfare bedroom, accumulates not only my own several piles of confusion, but several others. Estelle's curling irons are now in my card basket and Trueman's billfold and all his Hudson Guild stuff are here together with several papers and magazines.*

Trueman had railed at her with his troubles—bad luck with his radio, bicycle, school work, teachers and friends—and visited all his misery over these things on the family. "Especially as he is possessed to rail at me about them 'til he makes me cry, and he has nearly broken my heart several times lately. Then he too breaks down and reveals the struggle he is having with himself." Anita consoled herself by saying that she knew he was coming out all right. One night after a difficult scene, he surprised her by saying, as he was going to bed and she was starting to work on her sermon for the following morning:

> "Preach a good sermon for me, Mother, although I can't hear it. Seems to me that you always put something in your sermons especially for me." "Trueman," I said, surprised, "Do you ever listen to a sermon?" "Sure, I listen to yours, and sometimes I listen to Daddy's, but he doesn't take as much notice of individuals as you do."
>
> We have good talks about current events, scientific matters and abstract moral and spiritual problems, and everything which is impersonal. It is my job to be always prepared to lead conversation along these lines. Little sister is always ready to stir up strife, and for every ripple she starts, he makes a splash. So I am easily swamped if they get the start of me. Perhaps I'm a fool. I know I've been too indolent and otherwise absorbed to keep control, but I'm glad to have this experience with my children that I may understand other mothers.

Although Anita's diaries revealed more pain than joy, in one of the rare joyful entries, written in 1923, she exulted:

> My lover-husband drove me around Cape Ann, a beautiful trip. . . . our love seems almost too deep and wonderful to bear. No honeymoon could be so flaming-tender as these days of rich fulfillment: the children grown, the work established. Even some little gift of fame in our hand, won together, and so serving our love.

First Ministries:
Rowe Church and
Barnard Memorial

After her ordination in 1921, while serving as the summer minister at the Rowe, Massachusetts, church, Anita was instrumental in starting Rowe Camp. Several diary entries mentioned the germ of the idea for a summer institute. She spoke with various interested people, the Reverend Margaret Barnard—Rowe Church's former minister from 1902 to 1916—among them, of plans for a community church and a Connecticut Valley Institute there, from plans submitted by a Mr. Barker Hartshorn. Anita proclaimed that "[s]ometime my grain of mustard seed may shelter the fowls of the air."

In 1924 Anita was asked to serve another summer at Rowe; plans were shaping for a young people's encampment there that summer. In July, her diary noted that Rowe Camp was in full swing. Near the end of the camp season, on Rowe Camp Sunday, she wrote that the parsonage was very quiet now and she was alone, after a wonderful day that promised a successful final week for the young people's camp. She stated that there were over 150 at church and "how fine it was to hear them sing. . . . I believe the experiment is approved a success to a wide public." Everyone came over to the parsonage for their picnic, which proved "delightful," according to Anita. "How many gallons of our spring water they drank freely! Then the Sunday School organ was brought over and we had another fellowship meeting." The perfect weather had cooperated—a baking hot sun, but a delicious breeze. The trees seemed "almost loving in their shade," she wrote. Gradually the guests departed, some to the camp. Anita surmised that it had not been a burden to local people—that the success of it surprised them. "But the spirit is in it all," she said, "and I have faith, which added to the faith of others, will build an enduring installation here. Thank God for this beginning."

Anita reported that the program had gone as planned, with a camp membership of over thirty for the entire time; the conferences had been most stimulating; the young people had taken part eagerly—all attending loyally. The devotional services had been beautiful, and their chapel had grown into the affections of the youthful visitors. The trips had given them a taste of the variety and beauty of their environment, and the hospitality had endeared the staff and campers to each other. Now, at the end of the week, plans for another year were being considered. Anita told that the parish property was about to be placed at the service of the AUA for this work. "So it would seem," she rejoiced, "that my dream is coming true. I trust it all with thee, Mother Divine, and my part in it. Grant us to serve thy cause mightily in this place."

Anita wrote about a difference in attitude between herself and Margaret Barnard, her colleague. Anita's position was that she was trying to fit into everything, including serving on a supper committee, thinking that was much better than standing aloof. Margaret Barnard told Anita that she had made it her policy not to do "a man's work and a woman's work," so she left such domestic phases of church service as sewing and suppers entirely to the others. "It may be best for her," Anita wrote, "but having grown up in the 'woman's job,' taking on the 'man's job' of preaching and church administrator does not seem so ponderous a burden to me. If I fail to dignify the office, perhaps I can help to humanize it, and then I'm lucky enough to have Harold to carry the dignity end of it."

For a brief moment the rural splendor of the Berkshire hills inspired a few passages in her diary akin to the nature writing of the young Anita—rarely indulged in these later years, when life was taken up with the dailiness of her many duties:

Clear sunrise stillness rests upon these hills. Only the lowing of cows, the rumble of a distant train, the twitter of birds "embroider" the quiet. The grass on the slope, which leads up to Henry's corn field, shines with the dew which must have been almost frost. Magic threads and films of cobweb, the highways and the world of some small creatures, glisten a moment, made visible to human eyes by that same sunshine, which, licking away the moisture, makes them invisible again. What we know *is largely a matter of focus. A dozen worlds may be operating instantaneously about us, but our attention is tuned to a very slow one.*

While on a long solitary walk over the North road, with the solitude broken only by some distant cattle and an automobile on another road, she gloried in her surroundings:

So I lingered to really absorb the beauty of apple boughs crowded with curly crimson buds and chaste white blossoms, and of slender young birches with crisp documents reeling from their dark rolls of parchment. There was a shimmering gossamer silver shell on the outside, fragile as old paper, then a deep copper sheathing with the code spread over it in neat white dashes. This was split and curled away in places, to show the mellow gold of the living bark. I love these silver birches because they speak of my comrade, John Burroughs. There are white ones, too, virginal and proud, tossing their lovely veils of new green in the spring air.

A drift of white over the meadows, turns out to be millions of perfect little blossoms: bluets or innocence. This snow effect is enhanced by the white petals from the fruit trees. This summer I hope to get to know Rowe better than ever.

At the end of Anita's five-year ministry at Rowe, she wrote in a letter that the Rowe church was dear to all who had lived and worked with it, and that the five years of her ministry there were precious memories to her. She observed that some of her deepest friendships were rooted in those hills; that it brought her great satisfaction to know that her dream, growing in her heart those five summers, had so far found fulfillment in the Young People's Religious Union (YPRU) camp now established on a permanent foundation. She spoke of her hope for a Sunday School Institute there and other gatherings of Unitarian groups, using the beautiful chapel as a center of inspiration.

However, Anita deplored the lack of acceptance of her church in the Rowe community, writing that, on Old Home Day, after five years of service there, they were treated like strangers—"not even asked to squeeze lemons." She was told that one member of the community suggested that Harold be asked to speak, but was told sharply that it would "mix things up."

The chairman praised Baptists, saints, and deacons of the past, unblushingly. Finally he thanked the Unitarians—calling them "the congregation across the way"—for the use of their chairs, as though they were foreigners. Anita wrote that she wished she were not so sensitive, but she felt as if she could not endure another such celebration. "But let all that pass, as of little consequence. Our ministry goes on," she concluded.

An occasion of precious solitude was so uncommon for Anita that it prompted this entry: "A quiet evening working on sermon and service for tomorrow has been very peaceful. People do not understand how it is that I like and need to be alone." She then added that the work of the ministry is not done in the pulpit alone, or even chiefly. The privilege of leading in worship is the reward of faithful service in the pastoral and educational field. She declared that she would work harder on the Sunday School exhibition than on a dozen sermons.

Her diary saw a continuation of her conflict between her love for her family and her need for solitude: "Harold has been at home and so all the nooks and crannies of my busy life have been filled with his dear presence, as his companionship always pervades the whole of it." She bemoaned having messed up the laundry by leaving the basket out on the porch when a cloudburst came up, insisting that she was useless in practical matters. She pleaded:

> God help me. I ought to get down on my knees and scrub this kitchen floor—I must enjoy going over Colonial History and Elementary Arithmetic with my precious Laurel, instead of reading for my own entertainment. . . . Shall I ever be able to turn these [household] tasks over to someone else and earn the freedom from them which will enable me

to do well the work that I love? I suspect sometimes that my guardian angel keeps me tied to them during these middle years in order to restrain me from the strenuous life which would claim me if I were free to respond to its call. So, here goes, I'm going to scrub at least part of the floor.

Anita's diaries continued to record her ongoing struggles to balance her several demanding lives: minister, minister's wife, mother, lecturer, spiritual leader, feminist, peace worker, youth leader, writer. Probably the diaries were the sole recipients of these plaints. Certainly her daughters, when asked many decades later, insisted that they had not been aware of their mother's often expressed conflicts.

There are still faint echoes of the young idealist and romanticist in these entries, but they are modulated by maturity and life experience. Still she railed against the practical demands and the circumscriptions of marriage and family:

The dining room is converted into a study, pro tem, and I have been dropping into the professional attitude between jobs: getting out reports, planning calendars, preparing sermon outlines, reading—how I enjoy all this! Some day I promise myself I shall earn more time for this work, but I am very slow about my domestic duties, so that I'm barely settled at my typewriter before some other call comes and I must leave the work I can do best in order to blunder through the work that I'm not fitted for. Yet I love doing all these domestic things and hope always to have a home to do them in.

Anita fought the exclusion she suffered as a woman minister. People persisted in presenting her as the minister's wife. Once, when a colleague and his wife were with the Picketts at a party, someone remarked about having three ministers along. Another cried, "Three? Where are the three ministers?" and had to be reminded of her right to the title. "But the title counts little compared to the privilege of doing the work," Anita proclaimed. Her feelings about Harold's lack of support for her efforts surface again in these lines:

I've had to struggle with my old rebellion against Harold's plan of a joint account. I have earned more than he this winter and put it all into this joint account, then he takes nearly all of it and buys telephone stock in his own name. . . . [T]he principle is wrong, and I feel that I ought to protest for the sake of my sex in general. But I submit for the sake of peace. It is a situation which would drive most women to deceit and has tempted me to it. . . . If Harold would learn to speak of our joint endeavors as "ours," it would be easier. But I had to insist on being "the minister" at Rowe in order to have any standing at all and even when that was legally settled, I found that he was calling it a joint ministry, and then assuming, in conversation and correspondence, that he was really the responsible one. "Parson."

Anita wrote that Harold was proposing a joint ministry at Peabody, leaving him free for some denominational work beyond the pulpit supply office. "If that should come about," she wrote, "I must insist upon a definite standing and a separate salary, and I must have my own bank account."

Anita suffered greatly from the disapproval, whether real or imagined, of their parishioners. She believed that they had always felt she ought to do more in the church and "how I should have enjoyed it," she said, "but Harold would not let me until lately and now it is too late. It has angered them to have me away so much, and especially undertaking the Barnard Memorial work when they felt their own children and young people were neglected."

Anita agonized over her conviction that the parishioners had never liked their children and had been unkind to them. She felt that she had been criticized for the children's behavior and for her poor housekeeping, and, recently, for her extravagance in keeping a maid. "All in all," she proclaimed, "we do not fit." She wrote about a funeral in the Peabody church, where she and Harold held a joint ministry, saying that she felt a little twinge of pain at not being expected, as a matter of course, to take part in this service as joint minister of the church. Her rationalization was that there would be visiting male ministers, and Mrs. Hudson, the daughter of the deceased, couldn't be expected, with her traditions, to realize Anita's position in the community.

She continued, saying that she must remember that she owed her opportunities and standing in the profession almost entirely to the "loyalty and indulgence of her husband." If it were not for their partnership, she insisted, she would find her lot as hard as that of any other woman minister.[1] This rationale, more than any other in the diaries, speaks to her inability to see her situation clearly— whether because of her blind love for Harold, because of a lowered self-esteem from long years of marriage to him, or simply because that was the way women were expected to think at that time. It does seem that often she is trying to justify a nearly untenable situation with a certain amount of grace and acceptance.

In discussing her assignment at Barnard Memorial Church, Anita confided that this work would call for faculties she had failed to exercise. The woman who had traveled the country as a young fearless lecturer commented that she felt lost in the business district of Boston! "I must be alert and positive and personal," she avowed. "For years I strove to smother the personal, to be merely a voice of truth. In my traveling life, I made no effort to know people socially, to remember their names and connections, although sometimes I entered into the intimate secrets of their lives."[2]

She continued to berate herself for sometimes having mixed up names, "a deadly social sin," she proclaimed, for having offended many people by not recognizing them personally on the street, and for saying the wrong thing to the wrong person—as when she described a lecture to a lady who had attended it. "How could I have forgotten that she was there?" Anita wrote. "It is because my mind has been focused on the message rather than my hearers. I must train it to give full attention to personal detail. And if tact is simply kindness, I pray for a fuller measure of this spirit, and Oh, God, grant me skill in the art of appreciation." She prayed for a fluency in conversation as easy as her platform style, responsiveness, sympathy, and patience. She asked God to let her be honest with herself— acknowledging her faults, yet believing that the power to overcome them was with her—and that her prayer would bring forth fruit.

In Woburn, Harold had been asked to resign in 1922. Anita wrote that by his own admission he had neglected the Woburn parish work, that his headquarters work had taken too much of his attention. She added that even before he undertook that work, he was never very diligent about general visiting or the church organization. He regarded the Sunday morning services as the essential thing and felt the parish was so well organized that it could carry on other things without his taking the initiative. Meanwhile, according to Anita, "he has played too much, and while the particular group he was playing with liked it, others were jealous on behalf of the church or themselves." Then she learned that there had been some discussion with the parish committee before they sent the letter asking him to resign. She asserted that if only Harold had told her that in the first place, how much suffering it would have saved her! "I do hope he learns to be more frank with me." A few days later, she wrote that he was seeing the thing clearly and in a sensible way: learning its lessons and squaring himself for a more serious attitude toward his work. "It all brings us closer together." Anita sat with some other ministers' wives and talked about the problems they had in common:

> What is one to do? Condemnation awaits the minister's wife who is not an active worker in her husband's church, but if she is active, she is criticized for "running things." But woe betide the minister's wife, who being forbidden a sphere of service in her husband's church, gives such service outside his parish. . . . how I wish we might have two separate but adjacent churches.

In further comments about the Woburn parish committee's decisions, she declared that perhaps it was best that Harold didn't tell her much about it. She conjectured that the parish committee had been to headquarters and that the blame was being fixed upon her. "It has happened so before," she wrote. "A certain course of action has been forced upon me, then I have been blamed: not only for my own behavior but for the person who has initiated the policy. Must be my Karma to bear the sins of others as well as my own. But I accept it all and pray only that I may learn my lessons and not discredit the cause I would serve." Later, seemingly discouraged to the point where she considered giving up the ministry, she wrote that she would be glad to "shrink into my shell," to be just the minister's wife in some parish, as long as she could have a free hand in her own field "housekeeping, Sunday School or whatnot." Knowing of her lifelong vows of commitment to her calling, these sentences—"I do not care whether I'm winning recognition and earning a salary or not. The main thing is that Harold shall find and hold his place in the church"—don't ring true. If not pure rationalization, those lines at least illuminate the level of discouragement and depression she was experiencing:

> *The best comfort and discipline for heart and mind, in these days, is the memory of my ordination: Louis Cornish's words "Believe in us," Charles Billings' "Be a credit to us," and his welcome to the fellowship of all servants of truth, especially the Master. But above all, the hymn of the occasion, "O Master, Let Me Walk With Thee." Every line of that brings strength and peace. Thank God for such hallowed memories, crowned by the prayer from my dear husband's lips and heart. "Ebb, ocean of life, the flow will return."*

The occasions were infrequent indeed when Anita enjoyed a touch of her former fame, but she obviously felt pleased at such a moment when speaking at the Alliance in Lawrence. She reported that some New Thought people were there who heard her give her first address in Boston, at the New Thought Convention in Lorimer Hall 25 years ago.

On August 25, 1924, her diary once again was the friend with whom she shared her frustrations, wondering if she would ever be able to command leisure and privacy:

> *Creative impulses surge within me but they have to issue in apple pies. Only by pretending to take a bath and so securing the solitude of the kitchen and a lamp to myself have I been able to steal this hour of quiet and get off a couple of overdue letters.*

On August 31, a day of unprecedented leisure inspired her to record that it was her first vacation Sunday in four years. Harold was preaching in the lovely old meeting house in Peabody, and Margaret Barnard was preaching at Rowe. During this quiet hour before church, sitting comfortably in "Dan," their Ford car, she was enjoying the "sunswept beauty" of Milton's famous trees. "One tall poplar sparkles merrily among the rest," she wrote. By 1925, there was a more upbeat tone to many of her diary entries, and she was able to write more positively about her family and their demands upon her:

> I feel almost wicked to be making this demand. My days and nights are brimming with love. It is because my son likes to be at home, and wants to be near me, and he is so charmingly affectionate, that my days are so crowded. It is because of my husband's passionate love that I cannot use the quiet night hours for study and creative works. It is because we have the dear home together that the tasks of homemaking keep my hands busy while my brain is churning over half-formed projects which never come, because there is never time to concentrate upon them.
>
> But all the while in these happy home days, something is shaping in me which will be my sustaining strength in the days to come, when dear voices no longer break the silence. There will be time enough for writing when the children have their own homes, and only letters can reach them. God grant that Harold and I may always have our little home together, always. How I treasure every hour remembering that, at best, always is impossible.
>
> So tremendous a love as ours has grown to be, is immortal and will build home after home . . . be at home in stellar spaces as well as under shingled roofs, ready for change yet ever more profoundly permanent as the eternal grows and shakes off the shell of the brittle temporal.

Anita rejoiced in a quiet day spent with Laurel, remarking that her daughter was so lovely that it was a sacrament to help her with her bath. Wondering where Estelle and Harold were, Anita wrote that it seemed natural, somehow, for them to be scattered—that they loved each other more understandingly when they were not all constantly under the same roof. "Thank God for this elastic togetherness."

In summing up her blessings, Anita wrote that she was deeply thankful for certain spiritual gifts of those days. She revealed that Harold had set aside part of their savings in her name, so that she could feel there was something to show for her professional work: "I care more for his doing it than for its being done," she proclaimed. She was starting to feel that his presence in the house need not interfere with creative work if she could only "create time" to do it in. This meant a new phase of their "precious togetherness." She chided herself by saying that it had been a foolish inhibition that had strangled every impulse to write and study unless she could claim real solitude. "How I love preaching," she declared, "but then I love my family more, so I'm willing to wait for more constant work in that field, and to keep on cooking and sweeping and mending. How fortunate I am to be allowed to tuck in a little of the work I love. God help me to enjoy the work I *must do* for love's sake."

In a subsequent passage, Anita expressed her gratitude for a few moments of solitude. She remarked that there had been visitors coming and going constantly throughout that summer, "which I enjoy, but without some moments of quiet I cannot be my true self. I find myself longing for the winter schedule with the children at school and Harold away part of the time. When he is near, my whole being is wrapped about and intertwined with his."

Anita claimed that, as the years went by, she and Harold grew into closer harmony, especially when they could be alone together. She still passionately wished that they might read and study together, but commented that their resistance to intellectual dominance or interference and their widely different personal tastes in reading made that seem impossible. The eternally optimistic Anita avowed that even that would come with time:

My work in our own church counts, but for sheer delight, the sweet fellowship of the home becomes dearer every day, especially the dear love of our marriage. Last night at sunset after driving from the Elliot, at home in Cambridge, across the lovely stretches of the turnpike, we paused on our favorite eminence in a quiet part of Cross Street to feast together on the beauty there. Clear flame blending to fiery green and then to azure, with the crescent moon and two bright low stars was the sky behind the lovely forms of the trees, delicate

branching tracery of the leafless birches, sturdy oaks still gold-
en with dry leaves, soft silhouettes of the pines.

This was such a scene as old married lovers can enjoy
together, touched with melancholy and crowned with peace.
Perhaps solitude leads to larger scope of cosmic emotion, but
such love as ours in the presence of beauty becomes more
intense and surely brings the divine very near. I think, too,
that our growing appreciation of the children is giving our
love a new channel of expression. Thank God for all these
spiritual values and the power of realizing them.

Lest the reader be lulled into thinking that all the conflict had
been resolved, there are still more passages such as this one to
remind:

My eyes burn with tears, for, again this morning, I went
through the old Sunday morning struggle with Trueman.
How he protests against being a minister's son. The intensi-
ty and preoccupation of the minister's household on Sunday
morning, by contrast with the relaxation of other families, is
hard for the children to accept.

One would think ours old enough to understand and
cooperate, but even if all the stockings were darned, and I
pressed Trueman's pants while washing dishes after Laurel's
birthday party last night, they contrive to think of a score of
irrelevant questions to ask in the hour before church, and if
they are turned aside, they attack the situation more direct-
ly, "Why do I have to go to church? Why do you have such
long services? What's the use of so much music? Gee, but I
wish I wasn't a minister's son. Sundays are such misery to
me, I ask a simple question and you don't answer, and if I
ask it again, you get sore. Gee!"

These passages, so prevalent in her diaries, chronicle the difficulty of leading dual roles. They illustrate the belief held by women
ministers in the late 1800s, according to Cynthia Grant Tucker in
Prophetic Sisterhood, that marriage "did tend . . . to abbreviate a
woman's ministry or at least compromise its professional character."

The surprise is not that Anita waged these battles, but that she persevered—in spite of everything and everybody who would discourage her—refusing to give up!

When interviewed at the end of their own lives, her daughters divulged their opposing views of Anita's mothering: Estelle, the eldest, insisting that Anita had been a wonderful mother and Laurel, the youngest, insisting that she had not been a wonderful mother for her. Laurel commented that she had learned to read upside down, looking at her mother's typewriter from the other side of the desk, indicating that she felt the lack of Anita's undivided attention. Sadly, although Laurel was initially thrilled and supportive of the writing of this biography—in fact, thanked this writer for "bringing my mother back to life"—she expressed ambivalence, in the last interview before her death, about whether it ever got written or published, in what seemed to be a flash of residual anger at her mother.

Anita had read two books of memoir that prompted her to keep a closer record of the passing days, knowing that someday it would be her task to tell her own story and seeing how difficult it was when one tried to recall events thirty years later.

The joy and forgiveness in her heart sang out from the page when she wrote that Harold had been asked to go to Meadville to give some lectures for the students. "What a delightful thing this is after these years," she rejoiced, "I hope the day will come when we shall return to Woburn in triumph, and I shall not be satisfied 'til we have made good in Boise. After all, mistakes and failures help to build our lives and to fit us for larger service." Her hopes soared, as she maintained that Harold was wonderful and that surely he was earning a place in the history of their denomination.

Anita reported that she and Harold had begun their seventeenth year together by sharing a beautiful Easter service, nearly double the usual congregation, with lovely flowers and music. "I think our people like to have us in the pulpit together," she surmised. While awaiting his return from a trip to Boston, Anita wrote: "'He's coming, coming, coming,' sang the teakettle, symbol of home. How eagerly my heart leaps to meet him."

The 1920s:
The Uncertain Times

As the 1920s moved forward, the Picketts often felt great uncertainty concerning their future lives. While still at the Peabody church, they were wondering where they'd be next: Trueman was hoping for Greenfield, where his girlfriend was; Estelle for Jamaica Plain; Anita for Concord. Anita testified that "we ought, with our age and experience, to be suited for one of these places."

Anita told of an AUA meeting wherein a committee report of an investigation of the "state of the unsettled minister" severely criticized the secretary of the pulpit supply committee for allowing settled ministers to preach outside their own churches. Whether reference was actually made to the Picketts, or whether Anita only imagined it, we don't know. We only know that it confirmed her fear that she and Harold were resented for doing supply work, in addition to their pastorates. It prompted her to write, "I hope Harold will hereafter avoid suspicion on this ground. They do not know how much we have done as a labor of love. So far only once have I preached as a supply sent from headquarters. But they do not understand this. They do not know that I go only when a minister or a parish asks for me, and that when Harold goes, there is always an official reason for it." The report also stated that many ministers are unemployed because they are unemployable.

Anita's response was, "These are the very ones who criticize the office for favoritism." In Anita's candidacy for the ministry of the Dover, Massachusetts, First Parish Church, she was rather startled to hear that an announcement of her preaching was being sent out to all members; it was embarrassing to her to be so openly advertised as a candidate, and she objected, but in vain. "I am to have that experience . . . and 'preach it down' as so many of my colleagues have done. No resting on my husband's support in this case," she declared.

Anita dreamed of what she might do if given the opportunity, saying that the passion for preaching possessed her in those days. Sermons kept rolling forth in her consciousness and she felt that she could stir people "like any mission preacher." Preaching a Sunday sermon recently had given her a taste of what she could do. Themes, outlines, and phrases were running through her mind while she was cooking and washing dishes. She wished for the time to develop those ideas as thoroughly as she felt they deserved, and to follow lines of research suggested by them. As she agonized over whether that time would ever come, we hear in her cry the classic mid-life plaint "Is this all there is?" "And with almost rebellious passion," she lamented, "I sometimes realize that the passing of the years is leaving me out of the stream of culture."

Anita observed that art "except for homiletic purposes" bored Harold. She posed the question of how one could acquire a taste for art, even for such use, if one was unwilling—as Harold was—to spend time, money, and study to do so. She expressed hope that her children would grow to share her love of beauty, and contribute some creative work to the world:

> *I see the names of old friends wherever I look through the contents of a magazine. Shall I ever touch their lives again? These are great values but I would not exchange for them the joy of being needed by my children, if only to serve them in menial ways, and the privilege of creeping into my husband's arms at night. Time will bring larger meaning into our family life, but no sweeter ones.*

Several entries in Anita's diary in that year, 1926, deplored the passage of time with the changes it wrought—on her family, on her body, and on beloved old buildings of the denomination.

Anita divulged that she hated to let Laurel, her youngest child, go out in costume with some other girls at Halloween, but, since Laurel was nearly 13, Anita couldn't treat her as a baby anymore. "She still expects me to say our evening prayer with her as she goes

Estelle, Laurel, Harold, John, and Anita, 1926

to bed. And we shall treasure this sacred moment of the day, in fact and memory always."

She reported that she had been taking it easy, as her husband had instructed her when he left for Boston. "These are uncertain days for me with the haze of the great climacteric sometimes in my brain, as well as its depression and discomfort in my body. So I let many duties go by, and then attack them at most improper times," She wrote to her sister, Gertrude, of the effect on her of menopause:

I should have written to you before, but besides being very busy, I've been dull and hysterical by turns, as is the manner of "dames" of my perilous age. I'm getting through this uncomfortable period rather smoothly, I fancy, but there are days when I rather hate myself.

A visit to AUA headquarters at 25 Beacon Street in Boston prompted Anita to write of the changes there:

No successor for Dr. Buck [Florence] has been chosen . . . across the street the great brownstone blocks of 25 were coming down. It pulls at deepset heart strings to see those old walls disappearing. Channing Hall, with all its great memories and its abominable light arrangements, is no more, but the memories are ours.

It is transforming the neighborhood of Bullfinch Place Church, out Tremont St. by Barnard Memorial, the old rookeries are being displaced by handsome buildings. At this moment the ceremony of breaking ground for the new Unitarian Building begins. I wish I might be there, I hope Harold is.

A passage relating to the family schedule demonstrated that, even though the children were teenagers, they still presented heavy demands on Anita's time and energy. She rose before six and prepared breakfast for Trueman, who left on the 6:40 bus for school. Estelle, Laurel, and Harold came singly for breakfast; at 11, Laurel ran home for lunch; at 12, Estelle, Harold, and Anita had their lunch; at 1, Trueman arrived—just as Anita finished the dishes—and lunched heartily. Laurel was back at 2, looking for another bite. "So there goes my dream of a simple schedule for this year. It couldn't be much more complicated."

"And I don't know how I can manage with Harold around," Anita maintained. "Perhaps I'm too much of an individualist, but it is difficult for me to adjust myself to the complete communion which is my husband's ideal." Lately Harold had been taking the housework out of her hands a good deal and seemed to feel hurt if she wanted to be alone a little while. "How I treasure this tender affection of his. How I long for a fuller communion of our lives in all respects. Perhaps if I let him share the housework we shall grow into common appreciation of cultural interests. We surely have a wonderful community of spirit in our work, but I must, sometimes, be alone if I'm to be worth anything to him or our work." In another diary entry, she elaborated on her dilemma:

> It isn't any real help and it is very confusing, and it deprives me of that sense of detachment which has made these tasks bearable and the time spent on them a sort of spiritual exercise. I tried to get him to leave them to me and get out in the parish, but he persisted and finally explained to me that he wanted to share in my work, as he was letting me share in his. A complete conjugal communism seems to be his ideal, only in every aspect of the combination, he must be in control. He bosses me about the details of housekeeping, just as he acts for me in business matters, just because it is his nature. And after all, I submit because I love him.

Anita told of a recent Sunday evening that brought a severe test of their family affection. Harold had come home tired and irritable, and the children could not be kept from tormenting him. This led to a discouraging scene that "had its amusing aspects," according to Anita—with Trueman appearing in a new role: "defender of the quieter sex. Passionately he berated his father for laying violent hands upon Laurel, and was then obliged to defend himself." Anita declared it to be like an episode from a scenario. "Afterwards we all loved each other more than ever, but for a few moments all mutual respect vanished. I hope such a scene may never occur in our home again." And, indeed, if one did, it was never chronicled in her diaries.

In 1926, while still serving as joint ministers of the Unitarian Church in Peabody, the Picketts assumed a second joint ministry at the Medfield Unitarian Church. Anita's diary revealed that their being "joint ministers" was an arrangement that held up only so long as it was convenient for the "male member of the partnership." She had not been allowed to preach for over a month and understood she was to do so only when her husband was called away. "It's rather maddening, especially since I know the people want me to. I wonder if it is wise for me to submit. One thing is certain: I shall not, here or anywhere, do all the drudgery unless I have a share in the pulpit," she vowed.

The exclusion came not just from Harold, but from the denomination, reflecting the anti-feminine tenor of that period of time. She wrote that Harold was attending a meeting of the liberal ministers in Essex County to arrange an association.

It is hard not to feel "wrathy" about this being arranged to exclude the two women ministers in the county. I do not think the occasion will pass without some recognition of the error, but it is surprising with what consistency the brethren forget to remember us, even if they do not consciously ignore us. . . . I told . . . the host on this occasion, that I hoped my being in active service in the county would not embarrass the ministers about meetings . . . but he has invited "the men" to the Salem Club where women are not allowed, and I suspect that restriction is a convenient excuse for excluding us.

What really riled her, she said, is that Harold, in a telephone conversation, accepted the situation for her "with gusto," and then did not even take the trouble to tell her what it was all about. "He treats me in such a casual way about important matters," she wrote, "making and unmaking my arrangements without consulting me. I sometimes feel on the level with the charwoman whose husband feels he has a right to her wages, as well as all her personal services, and yet, he is such a glorious lover, I forgive all this, and accept his plans obediently."

In *Prophetic Sisterhood,* Cynthia Grant Tucker tells of the anti-woman stance of Samuel Eliot, who came to the leadership of the

AUA at the turn of the century. She reports that "he voted against women's suffrage . . . in Massachusetts and just as confidently opposed women having a voice in the pulpits. . . . Eliot's methods of operation and staffing practices made it clear that, in his estimation, women were poor professional risks, being creatures designed for private life and supportive roles and therefore naturally prone to abandon careers for marriage and domesticity." It would take more than that prevailing attitude, still somewhat evident in the 1920s, to discourage Anita. She expressed her joy and her philosophy toward her work in the following passages:

> How I enjoy pastoral work—this is what people need; the personal touch. Especially is it so with the dear old people who cannot go out. It means so much to them to be assured of our interest in them and to be told that they are really helping to build the mind of the world.
>
> . . . I find people want sermons of personal helpfulness most of the time. Controversial and sectarian sermons are useful once in awhile, but the most valuable service it can render is inspiration to its members.

At the outset of their joint ministry at the Medfield church, Anita had given up her summer ministry at the Rowe church and the chaplaincy of the Peabody Order of Eastern Star. She voiced a wish that now they could build upon this firm foundation—referring to their new ministry. She noted that their installation was beautiful and their work there already established. She observed, with pleasure, that it was the first time her own position in a joint ministry had rested on a parish call. In Peabody she had always had a feeling that the standing committee, although fully authorized, might have withheld calling her to the joint ministry—even though the decision was ratified when once made. She commented that there was no side current of criticism in Medfield. "The people want the joint ministry and like it and cooperate heartily," she rejoiced, "And I am 45. The travail and trouble of motherhood, together with the joys of its earlier phases, are built into my soul for strength." She wrote that the children soon would begin to share the financial burdens of their family life, would be building their own lives and leaving their parents to each other and their work:

For the first time since I have been in the ministry I am missing the Berry Street Conference and the Ministerial Union. Harold, I think, feels sensitive about his present position and doesn't want to have to talk it over with old friends. It makes me rather panicky to think how one after another golden opportunities have slipped through his hands: Boise, Woburn, the Pulpit Supply work, and now both Peabody and Bullfinch Place, while not exactly promising, are withdrawn in a manner which doesn't help our credit in the profession. Harold refuses to resign at Peabody, 'though he has accepted the wish of the parish that we terminate our work there September 1. How bitter is the pain of it.

He had also read our *resignation at Peabody. "My wife and I are now one, and* I'm *the one." He insists on my putting my Peabody salary check in the joint checking account and he wants to pay all the bills, even my personal ones, with joint account checks over his signature. I suppose it helps his sense of dignity. He says I can write the checks if I want to and take charge of the account. But I know that wouldn't work. However I must try to feel free with this account and share responsibility for it.*

Harold seemed to feel that this communism in money matters, as in household chores, was essential to their love. Anita professed her hopes that he would learn to share with her the making of plans and the sealing of arrangements that concerned them both. She spoke of having had a serious talk with him about it lately: that he now knew how she felt, "so now I must keep him up to it." She added that too often she had allowed him to make her plans and to take actions for her, when her "compliance was near obedience to his will." She felt that talking things over had brought them very close together spiritually. "We must build on this basis. We both have much to overcome and many mistakes to live down, but we have our love, our home, our family, and one small job between us."

Anita ended her ministry at Peabody with a final Sunday School Service, commenting that it was upsetting to know that there were plans to pay $2,500 for a single settled minister when the Picketts had been paid just $1,800. She explained that they were being allowed the summer salary in lieu of the raise they might have been given.

Harold thought it best that he should take the Children's Day service in the Medfield church, as there were to be some christenings, and "no doubt the people would feel better if he performed the ceremony." Anita obliged, saying that would give her the opportunity to preach the final sermon in Peabody, for which she was thankful.

Now that Harold had withdrawn all his interest from Peabody, his belongings covered her desk; only once in a while could she have the study to herself. She complained:

> *How I wish he would get some work that would take him away part of the time. There's not a spot in the world or an hour of the day that I can call my own. Soon the girls will be home, too, and, more than ever, every atom of me will be always under somebody else's claim. So, dear God, I surrender myself to Thee. Make me loving and patient and industrious for their sakes.*

In spite of her struggle to find time for her work, lectures and poetry were still a part of Anita's life in 1926. A note "from the hand of Elbert Hubbard" said this about a poem she called "A Mother's Prayer for Light": "All very sweetly expressed, with skill and fine reserve. Any one who can write as well as this should keep at it. We grow by doing!" In 1927 Anita wrote and published "Medfield Poems," and again, around 1934, a booklet of memorial poems called "Remembrance."

In the newspaper, the *Medfield Messenger,* the Women's Alliance in Walpole announced a series of Lenten lectures to be given by Rev. Anita T. Pickett in the vestry of the First Parish, Walpole, on Wednesday afternoons, starting on March 2, 1926 at three o'clock. The general subject was "Modern Religious Movement." The article stated that Mrs. Pickett would outline the history and ideas of Christian Science, Spiritualism, New Thought, Theosophy, and Community Churches. At the close of each lecture, there would be a free question period. It went on to say that the study of these movements would be sympathetic and show the more positive contributions each movement had made to modern day thought.

On November 22, 1926, while alone for the evening, she wrote that there seemed to be an invitation to larger things—a vast fellowship of great souls calling to her for whenever she could, for a few moments, "escape the clings" of her mortal life. She confessed that there were certain aspects of life that she longed to realize, but to do so she must "gently but with undeniable will divest myself of the holds that would hold me." Once again she bemoaned the fact that Harold did not share her love of art or her interest in Sunday school work. "If I ever get to see a real play, I must go alone. I keep promising myself that the children will share my tastes, but that does not satisfy my heart hunger. I want so much to share these great things with my husband. Will he ever awaken to their worth? I shall pray for it, and meanwhile I must not starve my own soul."

Anita continued her catalogue of complaints about Harold, saying how mean-spirited he was about giving gifts at Christmas, even though most of them went to his own side of the family. He begrudged the expense of driving to Boston with Anita and the children, although, according to her, he was quite willing to spend a whole day of his "precious time" driving another party's car.

She relates how enraged she was by the casual way in which Harold was invited to go on another trip with the Hamants, parishioners with whom he had formed a friendship, over the holiday, leaving her and the children to entertain themselves. He had accepted without consulting her, and she gave him a "piece of my mind," adding that it was not fair to the parish or the family that he should let these people, "dear and generous as they are," monopolize his time and attention. Anita was pleased that, fortunately, the weather was unpromising, so Harold had a good excuse to withdraw, enabling them to have a pleasant family outing. "He has been dear to us—took us to a show in Needham which we all enjoyed, and we had a fire in the fireplace and really treasured our home."

Anita objected to Harold's way of dealing with their finances, saying that when it suited his purpose he bragged about their savings and investment—even to the children—and yet made his family feel as miserably poor as when they were in debt. Although a good fair share of the saved earnings were invested in Anita's name, she did not feel that she had any right to them. "If I should use my own money without consulting my Lord and master," she said, "I should feel as if I had stolen it."

Once again, after venting her resentments, she came around to forgiveness, theorizing that "perhaps it is for the best of all concerned. Perhaps I do not interpret his attitude correctly." And during a time of sickness, she admitted her true gratitude to Harold for taking over the housework, saying, "God bless him for all his goodness, and forgive me for ever finding fault with him."

The couple argued over Anita's desire to help her mother clear her father's debts after he died—Anita proclaiming that she should have the right to use her own earnings for that purpose: "This bargaining attitude is just the thing that has spoiled Harold's professional career. The men who have made their way past him have been hard workers and generous givers."

She regretted that Harold did not get to succeed Dr. Eliot at Bullfinch Place. Her comment was that he had been considered at one time, but when it was found that he was planning to carry two, if not three, other churches, with her help, it seemed best to get someone else. She wrote that if he had only been willing to resign at Peabody, how much sorrow would have been saved. His trying to hold so many things led to the loss of all but this one task— Medfield, "so remote and inadequate." "But," she said, "we have this and we shall make the most of it. It is worthwhile as a task, 'though there is small promise of its ever furnishing full support for a minister without other income."

In order to make ends meet, Harold and Estelle worked in a factory part-time. In addition, Harold was making a name for himself as a "funeral parson." The Waterman Company, which conducted several thousand funerals a year, found him acceptable to their patrons, so sent for him when another minister was neither specified nor available.

Despite frequent complaints in her diaries, the following passage indicates that the Picketts had reached a more comfortable place in their marriage:

18 years! I remember when it seemed a long time to have been married 8 years. Now it seems a very little while and our marriage has grown to be so deep and rich that all experience is absorbed into it, yet we are amazingly free as individuals. Marriage is indeed a process, not an event.

The presence of a visiting friend from New York reminded Anita of her early life. She allows herself a brief expression of regret, quickly followed by a typical Anita rationalization:

Shall I ever get into that charmed circle again? So often now a touch of creative fire brushes my lips. . . . Perhaps there's no need of mine among so many voices, and I have my modest opportunity in our church work. Also, I must remember how, when I was rubbing elbows with artists and authors, my heart hungered for a house and for love and motherhood. No woman was ever more richly blessed than I am now in these things, but as my responsibility in these relations relaxes, I must press on to "the work" that calls me. There's no hurry about my calling, but I must not be too dangerously content with the comfort of domestic life.

Small wonder that, in October 1926, Anita wrote of feeling curiously depressed, but that she guessed it was mainly minister's blues. She reported that the children had been noisily protesting their fate as ministers' off-spring. "It is hard enough to hold a Unitarian church together, even when all one's strength and devotion can be given to it, but with the added strain of marshalling the family into Sabbath duties, it is much more difficult," she said.

Trueman had been dropped from private school. Anita confessed her unhappiness, saying she couldn't bear to think of it—"it is so humiliating"—yet she reminded herself that she, too, had dropped out of high school without graduating, and did not complete her course at Meadville or at Emerson. Harold had done a similar thing, both in school and in his pastorates. She went on to say that they had been lucky, but still the result was not what she would desire for her children. "At our age, if we had been more ambitious and *faithful* we should be in a much better position in life, but we are adventurers and perhaps we have garnered experience which is more valuable to us than conventional good standing."

We cannot do much for the children, but they seem to lack ambition anyway. We are a mediocre family after all— might as well admit it—and settle down to a meager but happy existence.

At one point, it appeared that they had been passed over by some people planning a funeral in their own parish. She agonized over it in her diary:

I'm used to being turned down because I am a woman—it always hurts but I understand it. This, however, is different and comes near being a direct insult. Though probably it is mere ignorance on the part of the family. Things like this are bad for the nerves of a woman of 45. [Later there were regrets and apologies and Harold was invited to speak.]

Anita described with joy a wonderful domestic day she and Laurel spent together when Laurel was about thirteen:

And this evening her dear flitting presence has not interfered with my work on my sermon. How I enjoy this . . . delving into books, sharing gathered material, adding another message to my collection. Can it be that hereafter I'm to have time and scope for this work?

On May 14, 1927, Anita, in Medfield for the second year, wrote to her sister, Gertrude: "I preached in three different towns yesterday." Also while at Medfield, Harold began working for the Society for the Prevention of Cruelty to Children for $1,500 a year. It would be a field in which he would continue working until his death. On March 14, 1928, the Picketts sent this letter to the clerk of the Medfield church:

Dear Mr. Wheeler, Will you kindly convey to the annual meeting of the parish tonight, a friendly greeting from the ministers who submit herewith their annual report together with the following observations: because Mr. Pickett has been appointed to a new and exacting field of child welfare work, and because Mrs. Pickett is still partially disabled by injury to her shoulder, and because of the discouraging industrial depression in the community, and because of the continuing and serious deficit in the finances of the church, the ministers would say that they are willing to accept or receive not more than $75 a month salary after April 1, until such time as the local conditions shall improve or their office with the parish be terminated.

Often the occasion of their wedding anniversary would inspire a kind of stock-taking of their marriage and of their lives. Such were these diary entries in 1928:

Years have passed, and how richly they have justified all the dreams of those old days. Was ever woman more blessed than I have been? The love I longed for came to me in the richest possible measure, yet did not separate me from the work for which I was born. The motherhood I craved has been richly fulfilled, bringing with it all the trials and joys of maternity. And now I am about to enter on a new phase of family experience, as a grandmother [to Estelle's first child].

Harold and I completed 20 years of our marriage yesterday . . . a precious day. In the evening, . . . we were walking about Needham [Massachusetts] in the spring twilight, when he spoke as he very seldom does, in personal conversation from his very soul. The spirit of content and completeness seemed to well up in him and express itself. . . . It was very tender and reverent. Mistakes of the past, he feels, are evil tendencies outlived. It is a great relief to have the children reaching the age of independence. He is such a wonderful lover—but not built for a family man. I fancy the next twenty years, if we are spared to spend it together, will be rich in mature romance for us. . . . [T]his year, Harold and I will probably be alone together, and no newlyweds ever took more joy in each other than we do. After bearing burdens together, sharing our work, facing deep personal problems, enduring great tragedies which almost wrecked our home, we have grown together gloriously.

Our work has been worthwhile, although we have not made a success in the ministry. At our age, we should be established in one of the large churches for life, but our restlessness and independence have made that impossible. Harold could not pay the price of progress in ecclesiastical preferment. He has found vastly more satisfaction in the social service work, in which for over a year now he has been engaged. It is a grind and pays but a small salary but there is room for progress in it.

Seven years ago, I was ordained to the ministry myself, and I've enjoyed my work in that field, but I, too, have grown weary of the petty problems involved in denominational service and parish administration. I'm hoping this year to get back in the lecture field. At the present time we are homeless, having concluded our last joint ministry in the 1st Parish Church of Medfield.

The Discouraging Years

In the summer of 1927, a long-time dream of Anita's came true when she finally went to Star Island, the Unitarian Camp and Conference Center in the Isles of Shoals, off the coast of Portsmouth, New Hampshire. She wrote of helping Charles Joy and Lyman Rutledge—her colleagues in the ministry—to build the beautiful stone parsonage there. She helped them load and unload lumber and build scaffolding for the masons, and laid a stone that "appears at the left side of the door as a brownish triangle about three feet above the sill. It runs well back into the wall, though it does not look large on the surface. A good symbol," she wrote.

The lyrics to a hymn were inspired by the centuries-old tradition of the silent lantern-lit procession winding uphill to the stone chapel that stands on the highest point on the small island—a tradition that is still observed nightly during Star Island conferences. The hymn she wrote, "Take Thy Light," may be found in the Readings section at the end of this book.

There would be many pages in her diaries before one again finds mention of that level of joy in her life. Most of Anita's journal entries in the late 1920s recorded a deepening of her discouragement and despondency. It seems that Trueman had gotten himself involved in a scandal (she never revealed the nature of it), and Harold was being criticized for unconventional behavior. "I do hope I haven't got to go through all that misery again. It makes one almost long to be free from the restraints of the ministry, and I do wish my menfolks weren't so demonstrating in speech and feeling," she declared.

She lamented that once more they had failed in the ministry, giving as reasons Harold's preoccupation with his work for the

Society for the Prevention of Cruelty to Children, her own disability (acute bursitis), and the indiscretions of the children, together with the financial depression of the town having caused the termination of their Medfield ministry on July 1. Harold had been appointed to the Brockton, Massachusetts, office of the SPCC, so there was some income coming in—"but it's a distressing situation," Anita proclaimed.

> *April 1—Two years ago this Sabbath, I began our work here. It has been a queer experience. Today I am utterly cast down. I don't see how I can live through the coming three months. Though we have many friends, they regard us with pity, and on every hand I encounter criticism of ourselves and our children. The worst thing about me is my inability to remember names and a devilish complex which makes me mix up people and names.*

Anita related a story of having called someone by the wrong name, whereupon the woman flew into a rage and accused her of never coming to see them, "so it's not surprising you don't know us!" Anita denied the accusation, but admitted that in two other cases lately, she had failed to recognize people—"an unpardonable sin in a minister, yet how little it has to do with the real work of the ministry and how hard people do make it." She complained that after the entire parish was presented en masse at a reception, the minister was expected to know everybody. "I have been remiss, I know, but not intentionally," she wrote. "In a small parish of my own, where I might make my own plans and my own mistakes, and then take my own punishment, I believe I would do better."

In May 1928, a diary entry reflected her thought that the angel of the Lord was turning her away from the ministry. She said that she knew she could preach, but could not carry on parish work. "I shall be happy when I'm free from it—I still feel that I'm a failure in this field."

The May meetings were a curious mixture of pleasure and pain for her that year. Everywhere she went, she heard the report of Harold's leaving the ministry, so began to feel rather outside of all the ministerial circles. One episode had been particularly trying, when Harold ("as usual," she said) wanted to leave in the middle of it, losing his temper when she lingered to talk with old friends. Anita remarked that he had grown really bitter toward the whole church connection. Coming home, life seemed for a while to be "a wreck"; her part in the progress of the family seemed to her to be merely endurance—so many dreams shattered, so many ideals unrealized, their work gone, their children content with mediocrity, and now their home to be dissolved. "What comes next?" she asked. "Let it come."

On May 30, Anita wrote that the day before had been the seventh anniversary of her ordination, and that she supposed that she would miss preaching, but at present was glad to be retiring for a while from the ministry. Even as she faced leaving the ministry, her calendar continued to be overly full. On a quiet day at home after a series of busy ones, she listed her week's many activities: entertaining two church organizations at their annual meetings; "attending upon" a mammoth rummage sale; going to Boston, via Brockton, to make some parish sick calls there as well as lunching with a friend; and hostessing a church picnic driven indoors by bad weather. On Sunday she preached and took part in Sunday school as well as a union service in the evening. On Monday she went for the first time in months to a ministerial union meeting. Suffering from a "furious" headache, she then joined her daughter Estelle in the task of finding suitable maternity garments:

> [It was] a thrilling experience for me as for her. She is quite unashamed of the fact that her motherhood is a little premature and so delighted with the prospect, that I can't help sharing her joy. God bless her in all things. She has chosen her path and her mate [Byron Coggins]. . . . It will be fascinating to watch and help her deal with the problems and experiences before her. Tomorrow I shall have a full day: service and sermon, Sunday School, hospital service, Townsend fellowship. I need solitude to prepare for it. . . . I suppose the lust for solitude is just as reprehensible as any other appetite. Certainly my hunger for this luxury meets many rebuffs.

During one summer, right after leaving the Medfield church, Anita burned many of her journals. "For awhile," she said, "I had moods of wanting to break with the past utterly, but that cannot be done." Despite her recurrent complaints of unfulfilled dreams, during the time that the Picketts lived in Brockton a promotional folder listed these available lecture topics by Anita:

Love and Labor	American Culture
Moving Mountains	Interwoven Worlds
Cosmic Motherhood	Economy and Wealth
Where Is Liberty?	The Circle of Silk
Palaces and Prisons	Lights and Lanterns
Fireworks and Flowers	The Pursuit of Happiness
The Psychology of Success	Keeping Up with the World
Our First Line of Defense	Fingerprints and Autographs

Some reviews from that same period were from "Prominent Club Presidents":

Mrs. Pickett is a speaker who makes interesting any subject which she may take. She is a deep thinker and expresses her thoughts clearly and poetically. Her lectures always give one food for thought, and clubs will be fortunate in securing her services. —Susan L Ferguson

It has been my privilege to hear Mrs. Anita Pickett a number of times, and I consider her a speaker of unusual power. As the result of a varied experience, a broad culture, and a depth of understanding of life and human nature, her message is always an interesting one, presented in a clear, complete, and artistic manner. Among the qualifications which make her an especially pleasing speaker are her excellent voice, clear diction, and choice English. —Lottie A. Leach

The all-time crowning review of her speaking ability, however, came from the pen of Elbert Hubbard, founder of Roycroft, who had written, sometime before 1915:

Anita Trueman Pickett is the most effective woman orator of whom I know. She thinks on her feet, and her expression is calm, poised, deliberate, limpid and lucid. She neither screeches nor purrs. She does not tear a passion to tatters. She convinces—and she convinces more by what she is than by what she says.

When Estelle graduated from Proctor Academy in Andover, Massachusetts, Anita gave the commencement speech address. Estelle grumbled that everyone complimented her on her mother's address and no one mentioned her own salutatory! Anita volunteered that Estelle's speech was excellent.

Meanwhile, her children continued to mature and reach for independence. She said of Trueman, "[T]he tall figure of my son appeared, swinging up the walk, his eyes full of dreams. . . . . He is trying to write a story and wants me to read it at each drafting. Yet I dare not criticize his work or offer a direct suggestion—for his great aim is to be original—and besides he is so easily discouraged, I can only 'nourish' his efforts in a maternal way. God help me to be the companion he needs in these last days of high school."

A step in Anita's own independence was her acquisition of a driving license in 1929, when she was forty-eight. She commented that she was learning to drive faster, climb hills, drive at night, back up, and park. "Such a joy it is to be independent in getting about and to be able to help others as so many have helped me."

In recent years, Anita's granddaughter, Carol Powell, related the tale of her grandmother being pulled over for speeding—Anita loved to speed, driving at seventy to seventy-five miles per hour at a time when there were no superhighways and the roads had many curves—and with all innocence and charm and big blue eyes telling the officer that she was clergy, and going to a funeral. Carol said, "He would say 'OK, lady,' and I never knew her to get a ticket or a fine."

The summer of 1929 found Anita at Tremayne, her family's farmhouse in New York State, which she hoped to make into a profitable bed-and-breakfast. In the Tremayne journal, Anita mentioned that she also had a dream of someday turning the stone house into a retreat for professionals. Years later, in 1935, Anita wrote a letter to Harold from Tremayne revealing her undying hope for those plans. She began the letter by saying that she had built her being into that place, that it was part of her, and that she longed to stay with it and build it into her dreams. She voiced the hope that the children would care for it as time went on, but if they didn't, her hope was that it would be made a "rest home for brain workers." "You made me very deeply happy yesterday," she wrote, "when you said we will plan to keep it. I do hope the time will come when you will enjoy it as much as I do."

In 1929, Gertrude, Anita's sister, then in her mid-forties, had gone off to New York City, hoping to seek her fortune and find a husband:

> *Gertrude is at the church where her "flame" is an usher. For once a human interest shares her mind with the wordy abstractions of Christian Science. May it enrich her soul no matter how the romance develops, but I should rejoice if she might find fulfillment of her long-suppressed womanhood.*

When Anita's efforts to start a bed-and-breakfast seemed destined to fail, she began to explore other avenues of employment. She wrote to the pulpit committee of the Norton, Massachusetts church. "A letter today from the chairman of the Norton parish politely closes that door and I shall make no further effort . . . in the Unitarian church," she declared.

On December 10, 1929 her diary disclosed that she had applied for a job as an agent for the Society for the Prevention of Cruelty to Children. "How foolish one of these questionnaires makes me look," she observed. "No education but unlimited capacity to learn, combined with maturity and wide experience may serve as well. At any rate, if they refuse me, I shall lose nothing. Harold seems to think me fitted for the work." Anita added that a Mr. Lothrop was excessively curious about her education and domestic responsibilities. It would be hard for her to take the aggressive and intrusive attitude that the work at times required, she said, "but when it is for the sake of abused and neglected children, it must be done, and I can do it in a friendly spirit."

Harold was preaching at the Brockton church and Anita rejoiced for him. A hint of the old romantic and poetic Anita came through in this passage from her diary:

> *Yesterday afternoon I went with Harold on a tour of duty which ended just at sunset in Duxbury. We drove out across*

the long bridge to the beach. There was a sunset of copper and bronze, lit by the ambers of a great hearthfire. The shore, with its architectural silhouette set off by the shapes of stately trees, stretched its dark strip between the upper and the nether fires. Then the crescent moon shyly appeared at first barely visible against that flaming sky. . . . [T]all trees framed the evening sky with its fading colors and more ardent moon. Lovely to ride thus with my lover and to come to our little nest, reaching our love to our scattered dear ones, and thankful that we, too, can spend these nights and part of these days together.

Anita voiced mixed feelings about her work in a diary entry in February 1930, shortly before a call came from the Unitarian Church at Barnstable, Massachusetts, returning her to the ministry. She noted that she had recently had a taste of the old life that sometimes seemed to be lost forever. She professed her contentment with quiet days—that they fulfilled some old longings of her spirit—insisting that she enjoyed being the dependent wife, felt that her life was now complete, and that she might just as well end on this note of peace.

However, in the very next sentence, as so often was the case, she wrote wistfully of her work—the work that she came into the world to do—saying that she could not accept that its only value had been in her youth:

When I see how hungry people are for the ministry of eloquence which sets their souls free and transforms common life into magical adventure, I feel that my gift is not dead. Give me but the opportunity and again I can stir the souls of men and women. I await the call. It must come that way. Every time I have tried to force my destiny, I have failed. My ministry must be broader than any church and untrammeled by any system. It must be of the spirit even if never again it finds voice.

The years from 1930 to 1935 found Anita settled into the ministry at Barnstable, and Harold presiding at the church on

Nantucket—an assignment he could not have taken without a "wife to run the Sunday School and to be his hostess" were it not that his eldest daughter, Estelle, was willing to move her husband, Byron, and family to Nantucket and assume that role. The Picketts often exchanged pulpits, and found time to be together in between their duties, but an absence of angst in her diary excerpts during those years would lead one to assume they were happy and fulfilled times for her, no doubt at least partly because she had her own separate church.

Perhaps Anita felt less need for keeping diaries during those fulfilling years, or they were burned or lost, for there is a long gap in the available records of 1934 to 1943. A journal does tell of a trip to England around 1934—Anita listed, in her preaching dates, two sermons in Birmingham, England. After her ministry in the Barnstable, Massachusetts, Unitarian church ended in 1935, she served the Bedford, Massachusetts, Unitarian church from 1937 to 1942. In 1943, after a year of association with the Dighton, Massachusetts, church, she was joyful when Harold told her that the church leaders had intimated that they would like the parish to make her co-pastor. She commented that it demonstrated, once more, what she had learned long ago—that one must achieve contentment before "the doors of life open to us." For a long while she had fretted about giving up her work and wished that she could "leave Sundays out of the calendar."

She wrote, "I had no technique for the position of minister's wife and did not want to do parish work without professional standing." She remarked that Harold had been very dear, patient, and understanding about it. An old issue, obviously never resolved between them, surfaced in the passage that said she had reveled in being her husband's wife and making a home for him, but Harold wanted to have his hand in everything—a move that she discouraged. To her, housekeeping was an art and she liked doing it *for* him rather than *with* him. She admonished herself not to be selfish about this. "Indeed," she wrote, "if we can achieve togetherness after these years of living and working separately, each strand in the pattern is precious. If I am to have professional recognition in the parish and my husband's confidence in sharing the work as well as our home, I shall be, as I am, a very happy woman and I must contrive more ways in which we can do things together in the home."

Anita wrote that their children had all been meeting hard experiences of growth—Estelle and her husband, Byron, struggling financially, and Trueman, now called Jack, getting into trouble at work and being branded as unfit for supervisory work. (He left there and found a position he liked better.) Always the forgiving and hopeful mother, she reported that his new position sounded important and more suitable to his temperament and ability. She expressed hope that he had learned the lesson "his experience should have taught him." Anita added that Harold was very impatient with Trueman, but she had reminded her husband that he, too, at that age, had been unsettled and independent, always ready to change rather than adjust himself.

The 1940s:
The World War II Years

The World War II years—1941 to 1945—brought some changes to the Picketts' lives. Anita told of the impact of wartime activities, saying that Laurel had been separated from her husband ("Gunny" Stackpole, from a well-known Nantucket family) for several months now while he was serving in the Signal Corps, stationed somewhere in the far North. Laurel and the children had been living at Tremayne for the duration. Anita divulged that it had been a difficult experience for both her and Gertrude, but that they had come through it well.

She wrote of Harold's training at Army Recognition Officer's School in Boston, learning to watch for enemy planes. She sometimes helped him when he was out on watch. She reported that Harold returned from Boston with a certificate as Recognition Officer and a snappy wings pin, having worked hard for the honor. "It entails a lot more work as he must now teach the rest of us," she related, "and he's none too sure of some of the nomenclature." Sharing in this activity—airplane observation—evidently gave Anita much pleasure, proving to be one of the rare mutual interests that she and Harold had discovered. "We had a precious day at the post Friday—no planes as it was raining, but we had a visit from two army inspectors and our district director. We are studying the shapes and gradually learning to identify them." They both worked on the Red Cross Roll Call, worked at getting subscriptions, went to rallies, and organized the campaign for Dighton—their charge.

Anita went to an Alliance meeting while in Boston; she wrote that her talk went very well and that it was good to be speaking again—"it is what I was built for!" During a ride to visit friends in Bristol, Anita was prompted to remark that, although the ride was delightful, she and Harold had little to say:

> *I notice we are pretty* dumb *when riding. I must find things to talk about and practice conversation. Also I must be more alert about information and accuracy. He takes me up on it though he also is given to exaggeration and flash judgments.*

She continued her litany of complaints about her husband, then—in characteristic Anita style—excused and forgave him. One has to question whether she needed to do that for her own peace of mind or whether she feared he might read her diaries.

One passage related that Harold had gone off on the early bus for an all-day jaunt, including a card party in the evening, falling back on his old habit—failing to tell Anita of his plan until he was on his way. Later, she reported that he found fault with how she squeezed the oranges and that he got down the "verboten" cup for his own coffee and none for her. "But I know now," she explained, "that this tendency is just an old habit which he is really trying to overcome. He's been so loving and appreciative lately that he's made me very happy."

Harold relayed to her that there was general approval of Anita becoming associate minister with him at Dighton, Massachusetts. This was not the first time she had heard rumors of that possibility. "It is a little humiliating," she wrote, "to have it going on without my being consulted, but humility is what I need, not the hurt kind, but 'a spirit of rational, filial, strong, unreserved, triumphant glad obedience'—in the words of yesterday's Lenten prayer."

She reminded herself that she had been content to give up her work altogether, "so if a little of it comes back to me, even in a left-handed fashion, I am most grateful." She continued on, saying that she had been forced to give up the expectation of her well-earned pension, so even if this irregular kind of a secondhand call was not to be recognized at headquarters, she felt she must accept it for itself. "God help me to do it gracefully, in triumphant glad obedience. And if nothing comes of it, I'm still content with my lot as my husband's wife if I can keep him happy."

Harold showed her a letter he had written, approving the idea of her becoming his associate here and giving his personal opinion that it should count toward her pension. "Funny how this proceeds," she wrote, "I've had no direct intimation and it would be easy to demand a more businesslike approach, but let it ride. . . . I have told Harold that unless they mean to give me a stipend, it must be understood that either of us can preach elsewhere on occasion. At any rate, I am to preach for the Union Service at our church Sunday evening."

Anita wrote that it seemed queer to have Easter morning without any spring raiment—her clothes were "tired" and she was indifferent to them. She commented that it was patriotic not to spend much money on them, and that her newest garment had already been a year old the previous summer. "May meeting's coming, too," she wrote. "Dear Harold's been pushing through my election as his associate so that I may attend the meetings as a ministerial delegate." On Easter Sunday, 1943, a parish meeting was finally held at which she was elected associate minister:

> But strange to say, my partner proceeded at once to arrange his May calendar without giving me any part in the program except to talk to the children on one of the five Sundays . . . He has changed it to include my preaching on the 23rd . . . [and] installation after church on the 16th.

During that week the Picketts spent the afternoon doing airplane observation together, and, in the evening, Harold went to a card party and Anita printed the calendars—"a big job. Worked 'til past midnight." A sample calendar exists from that time, and illustrates why it took so long: she used her skill as a photographer to make true "photo" copies for, presumably, the entire congregation!

On May 6, she told of attending the Channing conference the day before, "with a good delegation." She reported that "Fred" Eliot [Frederick May Eliot, president of the AUA] spoke splendidly and the Picketts had a good chat with him. Her call to the Dighton church was announced as an item of news. "It has been so good to go out in my own right as joint minister to make calls," she wrote, "and Harold has been glad to have me do so. Now I must work on my sermonette for next Sunday. . . . Monday, May 10—Yesterday Harold and I conducted our Mother's Day Service jointly."

As her journal entries became fewer, Anita wrote: "The most significant days take all time and attention so they do not get recorded—not easy to remember later." She skips about a month during which she said that her installation was May 16th, but the attendance was slim.

In reporting on the May meetings in the Arlington Street Church, she noted that there were some speeches that did not impress her, but these did:

> *Jacob Trapp of Denver dwelt on the dignity of man with many appeals to Emerson, Channing, Parker, and Whitman. Very poetic and mystical, yet stirring toward action—we sang his hymns.*
>
> *Vivian Pomeroy spoke dramatically of communion and community, even made us laugh, which by this time we needed, for many were uncomfortable from being so crowded and sitting on camp chairs or the high-side seats. He is enchanted by the idea of being possessed by the spirit. He thrilled us with his story of the Unitarian captain from Boston killed in the African landing and the passage marked in his testament "this is my body broken for you." We were much impressed by the chaplains among us and their testimony. They are indeed doing a great work. There was a brave effort on the part of the pacifists to stampede the annual meeting into declaring against the war and advocating peace without victory. But after a respectful hearing, the delegates voted them down. We made history by having the Ware lecture given by Dr. Walter White, president of the Society for the Advancement of Colored People and passing a resolution acknowledging their equality.*

Anita spoke of preaching in the morning at "our church," then giving an address at North Dighton in the evening, about which she said, "Might have been much better as to content, but somehow I got the attention of the 400 people. Enjoyed this."

In July, while Laurel's husband underwent surgery, the Picketts took care of David, their grandson. Anita spoke of how sweet he was and bright, but very shy and timid. He wanted to do everything with them and was never naughty, but Harold had no patience with him. She said that they were too busy to give him constant attention—"at least I am. Harold spends so much time reading—I wish he would try sharing life with this keen young soul." Laurel had taken the other children to stay with Gertrude at Tremayne, and Anita expressed her annoyance that, after leaving David with them, Laurel had taken two extra children along with her and her two daughters. "Harold has been nearly frantic with just David around. But poor Gertrude is expected to keep her poise with five of them," Anita wrote, and "Meanwhile I must preach on 'Conquering Chaos.'"

She wrote that the sermon had gone well, thus fortifying her for the challenge of this week. It seemed to modify Harold's attitude toward David, too. "I do share Harold's eagerness to get him off our hands. . . . Our quiet life together with home, garden, and church work just suits us." There was a long break in Anita's diary right

Anita at Tremayne in 1944

after she spoke of how their home was constantly filled with family members.

In May 1945, after supplying the Eastondale church for several weeks, the Picketts were asked to take charge of it; Anita was made the minister, with Harold as associate. She revealed that she had enjoyed the experience and it had added to their income. In 1946, she wrote that she expected to begin drawing her pension, but that was never confirmed until several years later, in her records.

In February 1947, Anita proclaimed her belief that the future of the AUA was in jeopardy from a "witch hunt for communists." She added that they had been made to "live down unwise behavior on the part of some of our representatives." She declared that a neighboring minister from Taunton, Massachusetts, had launched a campaign to discredit the administration and to "tie the fellowship to his own backward theology and lack of interest in the social and economic application of our gospel." He reportedly was using the whip of money to do this, urging people—even those in the Picketts' parish—not to contribute to the United Appeal. In a final volley of indignation, Anita remarked that "he never hesitates to come into our parish for weddings and funerals without consulting us."

On March 9, 1947, a joyful entry affirmed that the call to the Ware, Massachusetts, church was unanimous, so they were moving to Ware on April 29:

> *Each day sees some preparation while we carry on our planned work here and at Eastondale [Massachusetts]. It is such a relief to think of having a suitable house and the salary is adequate, too. Our income will not be quite as much as we have earned together with the AUA supplement while serving these two churches. However, there is some prospect of extra preaching for me. The AUA asked if we could carry Brookfield [Massachusetts], also, while Howard McDonald is ill. . . .*
>
> *April 5, Easter—A wonderful Easter—perhaps my last in the active ministry and perhaps not. . . . My white gown*

fitted the picture and I gave them the talk on "White Raiment."

Recently, when granddaughter Carol was describing her grand-mother's preaching style, she said that Anita often wore a white robe—as a statement that "Hey, the rest of 'em are men, I'm a woman!" Carol added that with her white hair—white from an early age—she was striking, and that she carried the robe in a suit-case just strong enough and high enough to give her "that extra boost when she removed the robe, put it on, put the suitcase behind the pulpit and stood [her five-foot-tall person] on it."

In June 1947, Anita wrote that it seemed odd to be the minis-ter's wife, but that she was contented with it, if she wasn't expected to do too much professional work without professional standing or remuneration. She insisted that housekeeping in that lovely home—the parsonage—would satisfy her.

One has to wonder about that statement, for almost in the next breath she writes of a visit to the doctor in which he tells her, with what she calls brutal frankness, that her nerves are depleted, her heart is skipping, her blood pressure is high, and she is showing symptoms of Parkinson's disease. Later she wrote that the hyperten-sion was reduced and she was using a B-complex prescription and resting much more than usual.

She observed that she had been reading a Humanist anthology, *Man Answers Death,* which, according to her, aimed to banish the fear with which orthodox religion has invested death. "These have never troubled me," she wrote, "and I share the feeling that ambi-tion for personal mortality is vanity, but the Humanists have not proved that personality is contained between birth and death, or as Whitman puts it, 'between my hat and my boots.'" An anecdote illuminating Anita's philosophy came from granddaughter Carol, who had been working as a nurse in a state hospital. She reported telling her grandmother about a couple who could no longer recog-nize each other. One night the wife tried to take Carol's keys—in fact, tried to strangle her in a frenzy to see her sick husband. She was subdued, but the next morning it was found that he had died in the night. When Carol asked her grandmother how this could be, she answered, "There's more to you than the top of the head and the soles of the feet."

Anita's ministry at Eastondale ended on June 24 with a wedding ceremony in a crowded church, following a morning farewell sermon and christening of the tiniest member of the church family—John Douglas Benefield, twenty days old. This was to be her last ministry until she assumed her husband's role as minister in Ware, Massachusetts, after his death.

Alone Again

The matter-of-fact tone of Anita's February 1950 diary entry upon Harold's sudden death belied the intense grief she felt and would later exhibit:

> *He died Feb. 20 at sunset just after parking his car in the lot at city hall in Brockton . . . right after lunch Harold started on one of his "cruises." How he loved to set forth on the open road at the wheel of a car. Usually there were college affairs at Harvard or Tufts, visits to ministers at Hartford or Providence where he was working on the memoirs of an old blind minister (whose name I never learned). More recently he went to see Anita Stackpole [Laurel's daughter who had polio] at the school for crippled children at Canton. . . . At Brockton, he used to fraternize with his old friends on the police force and our best guess is that he intended to spend the night with one of them.*

In the letter to her family, Anita confided that Harold had made a practice of going away for two days every other week, seldom indicating his plans. She referred to it as "his kind of holiday," which usually included some hospital and other calls.

Just before six o'clock, as she and Gertrude were eating supper, the Brockton hospital called to say that Harold had suffered a heart attack, was not expected to recover, and was, in fact, dead when brought into the hospital. He had come into the parking lot, parked his car (one of the attendants reported that he was alive and looked natural) and told the attendant that he wanted to look over some notes before leaving the car. Soon afterward, they found him leaning back against the seat as if he had gone to sleep.

Anita had written directions to be followed in the event of her death, and, only two or three weeks before, Harold had written on the copy that he wished the same to be done for him. It advised that, instead of a funeral or any local memorial service, on the second Sunday following their decease, each of the churches that they had served as minister—and any other churches in which they had preached—would burn a single candle during the regular morning service as a symbol of their continued presence in the places and the work that they had loved. And if any friends would have sent flowers, let them instead make a contribution to the Unitarian ministers' pension fund.

That wish was carried out on March 5 in their own church, presided over by the Reverend Dan Huntington Fenn, head of the Department of Ministry of the AUA and minister of the Church of the Larger Fellowship. Anita was to comment, a few days later, that she had made a list of her preaching so that when she died the Department of the Ministry would be prepared: "If all those churches burn candles for me, how widespread the light will be!" she exclaimed. A letter to Beacon Press the following year proclaims that number to be 76.

A letter of tribute from Frederick May Eliot, former president of the AUA, reads:

> Harold Lionel Pickett, who had served many of our churches with love, devotion and a rare gift of spiritual insight, died suddenly yesterday in Brockton, Massachusetts, in his 67th year. For 18 years, he had also served with the Massachusetts Society for the Prevention of Cruelty to Children. His friendly spirit will not be forgotten. Faithfully yours, Frederick May Eliot.

Carol said that her grandmother lay on her bed for days after her husband's death, sobbing out her immense grief. On March 13, Anita wrote in her diary:

Sweetheart, I woke this morning, for the first time since you went away, without crying for my loneliness for you, but I'm crying now to think of it.

And a week later, on March 20, she related the progress of her grieving process:

Dear Love, a month has passed now since you left your tired body in the driver's seat of my car. My love follows you, as it always did, in your wanderings, but I must not try to hold you. Only I must let my little self be swallowed up in the Divine, where you are.

On March 23, she told of a wonderful letter from Palfrey Perkins, a friend and colleague, but she added that each note renewed her feeling of loss.

"It is quite impossible to think of you and Harold apart and of course you are not really apart now." How precious it is to know that our fellow ministers feel that way about us and how true it is, yet we did not sit together at meetings, I took care not to isolate you from your menfriends. Even your womenfriends never separated us, much as some of them tried. From time to time we've been separated by distance, and our fields of work have been separate, yet there was more fellowship in our weekly visits than comes from sharing the same room constantly. We had our tragic moments of violent disagreement, but they always brought us closer together afterward. And in the work, you honored me more than I deserved.

Jack [Trueman] has been here this evening. Such a blessing you have left me in our dear children and a letter from Carol [granddaughter whom Anita had united with Charles Powell in marriage at All Souls' Church in Washington, D.C.] presages still another generation. God bless them all!

Anita wrote this poignant poem to express her grief:

LOOK AGAIN

How can I bear to look at the little plum tree
where only last week we saw, we two together,
A flock of evening grosbeaks plundering
The dried brown fruit, scattering shards on the snow?
Now a fresh snowfall has covered the husks.
The branches are bare as my grief.
The birds are gone, and you are gone, my love!
Yet I must look at the tree, remembering
That Spring will bring rosy buds and crimson blossoms
Out of those brown, bare twigs, and melt the snow.
There will be fruit again, growing under green leaves,
And when the leaves fall, glowing in purple beauty,
Then, above snow, another flight of wings.
Our love shall be in all these lovely things.

She wrote this prayer in her diary: "Help me, God, now to feel more fully the great free togetherness my darling and I have built, and out of that, and this new togetherness of separation, to help needy souls and build thy church."

After a missing page in her diary, Anita wrote that she had the very gown in which he preached, rather worn now—but mostly in places that would be out of sight after she took up the sleeves. The handsomely tailored yoke fit her perfectly, she observed.

"Our Easter service was a rich experience, but my voice broke over the Easter litany," Anita confided. "[T]here was a solo following and I let the tears flow to ease my heart, then I was all right for the rest of the service." She reported that she had been asked to assume, temporarily at least, the ministry at Ware:

Tomorrow I am preaching. It is a great legacy you have left me—this settlement in Ware. To stay on for a year or so in this beloved home we shared so happily and take up the work where you laid it down, in the freedom of my own responsibility, even as in these three years you alone have been responsible. It was hard sometimes not to interfere or suggest, but I tried to remember that I came here as the min-

ister's wife and housekeeper. It has been the people who demanded my preaching occasionally and now they want me to carry on the work for you and them. I'll try to be worthy of the call.

In October 1950, she was pleased when the trustees of the Ware church asked if she would stay another year. "It is a deep satisfaction that they want me to stay." During this time she recorded a weekly radio show called "The Chapel" on a local station. In December, she gave the "pilgrim church talk for our Wareabout ministers. Walter Swisher [presumably a friend from their seminary days] was there and compared it to my lectures at Meadville nearly fifty years ago."

On December 29, Anita wrote in her diary of a strange discovery she had made. Harold's financial papers were in disarray, and, upon opening a blank book that began as a parish record, she happened on an astounding entry: Harold had loaned his secretary, Helen Johnson, $365 for her mother's funeral expenses on January 2. Anita speculated that perhaps Helen had repaid him before he died, but it seemed strange to her that he had never mentioned it. It led her to wonder what he had done with all the income he was collecting from his pension, his converted insurance policy, their joint government bonds, and telephone dividends. Their joint bank accounts at Taunton and Brockton did not explain the disappearance of over $2,000. She wrote to Helen to see if she knew of a third bank account.

On January 5, 1951, Anita noted that she had decided not to do anything about the deficit in Harold's accounts, after consulting with her attorney and corresponding with Helen. They assured her that he lost some money while acting as mediator in an adoption case that involved the transfer of funds, and did not loan Helen any—though he intended to, and entered it as fact in his records. After further thought, Anita was able to account for more than half of it—spent on the past year's vacation and on Jack's Ford and their own DeSoto automobiles.

The insurance policies were another puzzle. Anita remembered that at one time Harold was paying so much for insurance that they were strapped for current expenses. At her protest, he had converted one or more of them. "Must ask for a report . . . I've been losing sleep over these problems and that I cannot afford," she cautioned.

155

Although no other reference appeared in any of her extant diaries, her poverty in her last years indicates that the money was never found.

A final summation of Anita and Harold's relationship came on New Year's Day, 1951, when she wrote, "What a wonderful love it is that held us together through the long years in spite of all the people and circumstances that could have separated us. Always, after excursions into strange lands with other companions, you came back to me—not penitent, but confident of my love and faith."

On the first anniversary of Harold's death, Anita exclaimed over what a year it had been, with so many deep roots of long association to tug at her heart and tear it again and again—yet she declared that she had been richly content in her sorrow. She expressed her thankfulness that her "darling" had gone in the hour of his full strength and usefulness and that strength had been given her to carry on in his place. She prayed that she, too, might go quickly when her time came. Anita then remarked on two elderly ministers who had continued to preach—"it was pathetic to see them."

On July 5, 1951, she spoke for the first time of writing her autobiography. She said that she had unearthed a copy of the start of her biography, arranged her journals in sequence, verified some early dates, and written a couple of pages. She remarked that she got lost in the Meadville section of the journal with its story of the Picketts' courtship. "How it made me weep!" she wrote. She also read over her 1903 adventures, when she had gone so deeply into Catholicism. "How much my study of it enriched my soul, yet how thankful I am that the stars finally saved me from surrendering to that lure!"

On September 23, she wrote that she had been through deep waters lately, as the old malady—depression—crept up on her, because she overtaxed herself during the summer. She said that this time she must accept it as part of her life; good planning had kept it in abeyance during the past four years, and she hoped that proper food, medication, and rest would enable her to continue her work a while longer.

On November 17, her diary recorded that her nervous condition had been frightful at times; she went back to "understanding young Doctor Appleford," who gave her neurological tests that proved negative for Parkinson's disease. Her other physician, Doctor

Roberson, had given her medicine for Parkinson's. Anita claimed that it was worse than the disease. Her tension was relieved by walking, which she tried to do outdoors. Otherwise, she had to get up in the middle of the night and wear herself out walking. She wrote, "[T]he occasional real night's sleep is luxury."

Anita anticipated that traveling would soothe her nerves and that preaching would lift her above her infirmities: "Two weeks from this minute I shall be with my beloved fellowship in Baton Rouge." In July 1951, she spoke at Nantucket and Barnstable. The sermon at Barnstable, "The Best Is Yet to Be," was on growing old. In between, she spoke to the Juniors at Rowe Camp about the beginning of the camp.

Edward Darling was the Beacon Press editor with whom she dealt in the publishing of her book *How Luke Discovered Christmas.* She wrote to him of her concern about the bookstore in Ware, which was run by Catholics; his answer was, "Don't be afraid of Catholic antipathy. My guess is that they'll keep quiet about it, but if they become vocal then we'll sell a lot of books."

An entire scrapbook in the heritage room at Rowe Camp and Conference Center is devoted to letters about the publication of *Luke;* they bear evidence that Anita had lost none of her fire and determination, nor her perfectionism. One review of her book, from an unknown source, reads as follows:

> This little book of only 62 pages is both a notable addition to the treasury of Christmas literature and very satisfactory solution to at least one of the enigmas of New Testament origins. Moreover it is written with consummate skill in such a way that simplicity, reverence and sound scholarship are perfectly blended.

The *New York Times* review of December 15, 1951, said: "A reverent imagination has woven conjectural fiction around the great mystery." One of her last poems, "From Every Cradle," written in 1951, also dealt with the theme of Christmas.

On December 23, 1951, Anita proudly revealed that the minister of All Souls' Church in Washington. D.C., the Reverend Dr. A. Powell Davies, had printed "From Every Cradle," on the front of his Order of Service.

One of the letters to Ed Darling noted that Anita was retiring from the ministry in Ware on July 1, 1952. On May 26, 1952, just before her retirement, Anita gave the invocation at an AUA luncheon. Also in 1952, she wrote:

The old sense of deep content comes over me in quiet moments. I wake in the night hearing the Montreal plane go over, and glance at its lights crossing the sky, before I drift asleep again. The birds wake me between 5 and 6 and I intend to get up then and write for an hour or two before going down to get breakfast. . . . I have all my files, journals, etc., here, so I should be able to get ahead on my life's story. . . . Everything has fitted so well together that I feel the spirit is working with me, and that the means for completing the future will be provided.

After her retirement, Anita moved back to her family's home, Tremayne, in Kingston, New York, where she and her sister Gertrude would live together for many years. Her heart had remained forever linked to the lush green valley whose river and surrounding mountains had inspired her best nature writing. It was to this source of inspiration that she now turned for the writing of her never-to-be-published autobiography that she called "Grandmanita's Youth."

What a chore—it's almost like doing research on someone else's biography. It dazzles me at this distance to recall again the spiritual, social and literary adventures of those days. I went pretty deep into Catholicism, escaping from its control with a wealth of experience. I worked with the Spiritualists without compromising my own philosophy of individual responsibility. I shared the disciplines of Theosophy and Vedanta, yet preached my own gospel. I refused to wear any tag, but all the while I was building up a system of thought and personal discipline which fitted the Unitarian ministry. Someday it will make a good "How I became a Unitarian" story.

She spoke of her contentment at being at Tremayne:

A part of this completeness is the assurance that the immortal self of my lover is with me. Here, where we spent our first summer together, he is my companion in a freedom we could not know while earthly ties bound us.

While listening to Eileen Farrell sing "In the Gloaming," Anita felt as if the lyrics, "In the gloaming, oh, my darling, think not bitterly of me. Though I passed away in silence, left you lonely, set you free," were a direct message from her lover. She noted that she had found several, in looking through her journals. She explained that it was very hard for him to say "I love you," but he could write it in crayon on notes pinned to her pillow, and in his letters. We are reminded by these musings of Anita's early metaphysical leanings; they seem to have been, in her old age, still a part of her canon of beliefs. She also wrote that she had been through an exhausting period of mourning for Harold, brought on by reading over the records of their early companionship:

Even then, I held his wonderful love as a treasure left in my keeping, and soon to be taken away. If I had thought then we would have 42 years together, it would have seemed like an age. I found my poem, "Reverie at Dawn," in which I anticipated his death and thought of him as calling to me in this half-sleep of life, yet not fully awakening me. Even as then, I spoke his name while he slept, and felt that he responded, though he did not wake.

Anita spoke of her frustration at her sister Gertrude's unwillingness to visit people, saying that she, herself, would like to go cruising and visiting—discovering new friends and making these last days "as rich as my youth was." She told of how she had finished reading the journals, completing her "strange youth story," and now she must "get at the job of revising the original sketch."

And how I long to record the sunsets and other scenes of these days, but I do not feel free even to work on my book. She is so curious about everything. If she could only go away for awhile, but my only respite is to get away myself.

July, 1953—What a strange legacy my mother bequeathed to me and my sister! She [Gertrude] has swallowed the labor and achievements of my years without question, and I have invested savings which should go to my children in this home for her old age. Yet I feel homeless myself, for she resents every suggestion I make.

Anita listed all her problems with Gertrude, ending a paragraph with "Come back, my soul!" She spoke with sadness of what her life had become; writing that she kept on making meals, buying, cooking, taking Gertrude for a ride, and playing Scrabble with her each afternoon and Samba each evening. "What a life!" she proclaimed, "I wonder what comes next for me."

July 1954—A precious morning alone at the cabin, reading my journal of the momentous summer of 1907. What a poet and what a rebel she was—that woman who a year later was to find the fulfillment of her dreams, living in a tent down here by the Esopus where the handsome new camp now stands. Harold read this journal on one of his Sandwich trips and wrote a few precious pages in comments at its close. What a glorious lover he was!

I have been enjoying a vast peace while living over the loves and work of my strange youth. It is my withdraw [sic] into memory—my outreaching into cosmic companionship with dear ones gone into the larger life.

Perhaps while sleeping outdoors, "the entire summer on a couch on the porch and into September," she was reminded of her summer-long honeymoon on the banks of the Esopus River so many years ago.

December 31—The long year closes. How much indeed it has meant. Perhaps from end to end it has been dominated by the book [How Luke Discovered Christmas]. A year ago I was still revising it. . . . Now it is a widely circulated and well-received volume. I have no idea what the sales have been, but the reviews are good.

In 1953, while working on her memoir, Anita commented that she had made some progress lately, and saw clearly how it should begin and end—with a postscript Harold wrote in her last journal written before meeting him, "and this is the fitting conclusion."

And So It Ends

Accolades were fewer and further between as Anita neared the end of her life. Her diary entries also were fewer and further between, and became more prosaic—concerned mainly with health, finances, and the daily details of her life.

Upon the occasion of her retirement in 1952, a letter came from the clerk of the annual meeting at the Ware church, bringing thanks to Anita for all her services and regrets at her leaving. In the letter, she was commended for her courage in carrying on alone the duties of both a minister and a minister's wife. "You will be missed," the letter said.

A check for fifty dollars was presented to Anita at a luncheon meeting of the United Appeal, and a little note with it said, "From the 25 churches of the Worcester conference to bid you Godspeed and to say that we are not retiring you from our memories."

In January 1953, Anita reported that her pension check included an extra half-pension—a donation from some well-to-do minister, who was sharing his pension with her and another minister, to be sent each quarter as long as she wished it. The importance of this gesture to Anita is illuminated by her granddaughter's story of the appalling discovery—made by the family after Anita's death—of her desperate financial straits in those last years: Carol told of reading in Anita's memoir that she had set out on preaching tours to far-distant places without any money in her pocket, thus demonstrating her unswerving faith to the end.

In October 1954, an invitation came to the dedication of the marble tablet in the Dighton, Massachusetts church, on which both Picketts' names are inscribed.

The first mention of an effort to form a Unitarian congregation in the Kingston area was in Anita's December 1952 journal. She reported that six people met and planned for a lecture the following Sunday night. She went with several others to Poughkeepsie, for the organization meeting of the fellowship there, commenting that it was thrilling to witness the birth of a new Unitarian church. She bemoaned that on the west side of the Hudson, where she lived, there was no tradition to lean upon. In 1954 she wrote, "My inclination at this time is to settle down to spend the rest of my days building a Kingston Unitarian Fellowship."

Later entries chart the course of development toward the founding of the Unitarian Fellowship of Ulster County. She received a letter from Munroe Husbands, Director of Fellowships for the AUA, saying he might come to Kingston in November 1956 to see about forming a fellowship there. It would be two years before it actually happened—in 1958.

In 1959, Anita recorded that she and David Stackpole, her grandson who was living with her for awhile at Tremayne, were charter members of this newly formed fellowship and that she had served as publicity chairman during the first year. "I have refrained from any leadership except as they have discovered my familiarity with procedure and depend on it. But I hope they will make me 'honorary minister,' so that I may have ministerial standing in the community and as a delegate at AUA meetings. I did give a talk for them on the proposed merger with the Universalists," she wrote. Nothing was ever done about that wish, and probably her diary was the only outlet for her modest desire. Upon Anita's death in 1960, she willed her home to the then-new Unitarian Fellowship—now the Unitarian Universalist Congregation of the Catskills.

From 1952 to 1959, Anita preached in twelve different localities, at some only once, but at one—her beloved Unitarian Fellowship in Baton Rouge, Louisiana—she spoke on fourteen separate occasions. For a woman in her seventies, in poor health—she was diagnosed with Parkinson's disease and a blood disorder, probably leukemia, that required blood transfusions toward the end of her life—her schedule was daunting indeed. She traveled to churches in Yonkers, New York; Wilmington, Delaware; and Knoxville, Tennessee; and to fellowships in Galveston, Texas; Chattanooga, Tennessee; Columbia, North Carolina; Yuma, Arizona; Jacksonville,

Florida; Los Alamos, New Mexico; Bartlesville, Oklahoma; and Fairhope, Alabama. One marvels at her ability to accomplish all of that, when, as her diary entries noted, her health continued to deteriorate.

Anita reported on a visit to a doctor in Kingston who sent her for a blood count that proved to be dangerously low—forty percent—so he started her on a massive intake of liver, iron, and folic acid; injections given her by a visiting nurse. Memories of the founding members of the Unitarian Fellowship of Ulster County, in Kingston—one of whom was a physician who treated her near the end of her life—are that she had a form of leukemia.

While visiting a Presbyterian church, she said she was distressed by a bad attack of paralysis agitans, and felt that she had better not attend church unless she could be sure of a spot where her affliction would not bother other people. Her granddaughter, Carol, when asked to describe her grandmother, spoke of her "indomitable spirit and courage," her "strength, power, and faith . . . the faith that got her through almost insurmountable odds. . . ." In response to the question of whether her grandmother had changed over the years (meaning her courage, determination, and moral strength), Carol's reply was, "*never, never, never*—you could knock her down and she'd get straight up again."

Carol's comment about her grandmother's indomitable spirit and her refusal to give up could also apply to the Picketts' marriage. In 1928, Anita spoke for all the years, past and future, of their lives together, when she wrote:

Harold and I found our togetherness in sharing our work. In domestic and business affairs we can seldom agree. It was the work which brought us together in the first place and it was the work which healed our differences. Harold gave me my motherhood—the supreme thing in my life with its extension into two more generations. He is in those children, grandchildren and great-grandchildren.

Anita's rhetoric faded as old age and illness took their inevitable toll, yet her love for nature continued. Toward the end of her life, she wrote, "A garden is good geriatrics. It provides a mild incentive to continue living. I must be here to see my bulbs bloom in the Spring."

Several pieces of her writing sum up for us her philosophy. In the frontispiece of her copy of her early book, *Suggestions for Students of Psychology*, she added this postscript in 1954:

> *The time has come to reconsider this little book. Some five hundred copies are scattered in as many libraries, though I doubt if they have been read recently. The dogmas of "modern psychology" as announced by Freud, Jung, et al, have supplanted the simpler, more creative knowledge of two generations ago. I do not find that they change my picture of the self and its relation to the Universe, but they do explain the confusions and the frustrations of the person who is dominated by his subconscious mind with its knotty complexes and I still see that subconscious area as external to the true self, like the shell of a living egg to be dissolved or destroyed by the expanding inner self.*

Probably the finest piece of writing left to us is the following expression of Anita's faith:

A CONFESSION OF FAITH . . . Anita Trueman Pickett

To realize and reveal the Divine within my soul,
To see, serve, and worship the Divine in all else;
This is my life, my faith, my religion.

It is the Soul of Science and the Goal of Philosophy;
It glorifies all forms of human love.
It sanctifies service,
*   transforming Labor into Art.*
It justifies the delight of Man
*   in communion with Nature.*
It exposes Sin to the flame which consumes it,
For Sin is the SENSE OF SEPARATENESS which
*   crushes the Divine within,*
*   and hides the Divine about us.*
It explains Evil, which exists only for the
*   Finite Mind, because of its separateness.*

It overcomes Evil, by bringing the Separate Self
into union with the Universal Spirit.

The Divine Self has created within its Being
many separate selves
That in each it may enfold a revealer and a
beholder of its own perfection.
I am one of these separate selves, and I
follow my destiny.
Every day is a romantic adventure.
Every place I visit is holy ground.
All persons I meet are Divine Companions,
seeking me as I seek them.
That we may reveal the Divine in our souls
one to another,
And share the Divine that we discover
in our Universe.

Evidently the following letter—never sent, but found in Anita's souvenirs—was in response to criticism of her philosophies. The date was April 7, 1947. This letter, along with the previous statement of faith, defines her spiritual journey and tells the story of her life. To the editor of the ministerial union newsletter, she wrote:

Dear Sir, Perhaps this may help to quiet the fears Mr. Lawson stirred up in the last News-Letter. *He feels that he has a mission to "expose" certain systems of thought and programs of reform. My mission has been to explore them, find out why they help people, and weave their positive values into my preaching of the Unitarian Gospel.*

In 1907, I was engaged to give a course of lectures for the Metaphysical Club in Pittsburgh. I had worked out my own philosophy, and it was vital enough to bring together three mornings a week what would have been a respectable congregation in some Unitarian Churches. Dr. L. Walter Mason, of Sainted memory, attended these lectures, and invited me to preach in the First Unitarian Church, later arranging four special Sunday evening services for me. Reverend Lewis G. Wilson, then Secretary of the AUA came to Pittsburgh at the time, and attended one of the lectures. They persuaded me that the religious philosophy I was expounding was Unitarian, and that I should enter the Unitarian ministry.

In these forty years, besides raising a family, I have held three five-year pastorates in Unitarian churches in my own right, and have been co-pastor with my husband nine years, during five of which we have been serving two churches jointly. In addition, I have preached as supply or exchange 205 times in 54 different Unitarian Churches. So a lot of Unitarians have agreed with Dr. Mason and Dr. Wilson that I am an acceptable Unitarian.

But I am a better Unitarian because of sympathetic fellowship with human souls in many fields and phases of spiritual experience. I cannot forget my girlhood experience of working with my father in the Single Tax Movement, and consecrating my life to public service as I stood beside Henry George's bier in 1897. I treasure beyond words my excursion into Catholicism, under the guidance of a wise and friendly priest, who had attended and approved one of my lectures, and wanted me to understand the symbols and ritual of the Church, and to feel at home in her sanctuaries. I like to think of the season I spent with a Theosophical family, where we read the Bhagavad Gita at meals, and departed for the Astral plane when we retired. Once more I am sitting between two dear old Quakers in William Penn's own Meeting House and they are praying the Spirit to move me to speak, helping it along with gentle elbow nudges. I can even match Mr. Lawson's scorn of vegetarians by recalling an actual vegetarian church in Philadelphia, and they were certainly a robust lot of earnest and friendly Christians. A fourth-generation vegetarian among them was several times an athletic champion. I could mention a dozen other associations which have enriched my own religion and my ministry. Not the least is my appreciation of the argumentative type to which Mr. Lawson belongs. My father was that kind of a man. —Anita Trueman Pickett

168

Anita in New York, 1904

I am a child of God, My immediate inheritance is divine,
My immediate environment is Spirit,
I accept the world as my workshop, my heredity as my tool,
My environment as the raw material from which to make my
life a work of art that shall glorify God.
                              —Anita Trueman Pickett,
                                  epigraph to 1924–1926 journal

And that she most certainly did. The telling of the story of Anita's life—truly "a work of art that glorified God"—is long overdue.

I like to think that when she died on September 19, 1960, it was with the serenity that she expressed so eloquently in this diary passage from her youth:

And so, once more, my city, farewell. I hope I may steal away from the earth some morning, while it is yet asleep, my departure unnoticed, and drift down the river of Death as serenely as now, in leaving you, I float down my glorious Hudson.

Epilogue

In the end, I give you Anita Trueman Pickett, in all her complexity. Perhaps she didn't make the difference that she hoped to, and that her illustrious start heralded. She did blaze trails, and she did have an impact on huge numbers of souls in her long and incredible life, not the least of which were the family she bore—a family of children, grandchildren, and great-grandchildren who led good, purposeful lives: some creative in the arts, some vital in her chosen denomination, some in spiritual paths of their own choosing—all contributing members of society and all proud of their "Grandmanita."

If there is tragedy to her life, it is that she was nearly forgotten by the public that she loved so dearly and served so long and well. Her story might have been helpful to the women in the ensuing years who have had similar struggles and obstacles in their efforts to serve as spiritual leaders. Perhaps it's not too late.

Notes

All of the quotes from Anita Trueman Pickett (ATP) are found in either her unpublished autobiography, "Grandmanita's Youth," which is in the possession of several of her grandchildren, or in numerous diaries and journals, also mostly in their possession. Her autobiography covers the years of her life from 1881 to 1908, with some interpretation and analysis from her vantage in her seventies when it was written. Most of the quotes used are identified in the text as to their source—autobiography or diaries—so don't bear repeating here.

Additional resource materials—diaries, photos, sermon notes, and newspaper clippings—are located at Rowe Camp and Conference Center in Rowe, Massachusetts or at the Andover-Newton Library Archives at Harvard Divinity School, Cambridge, Massachusetts.

Anita's First Years and the Paternal Influence

1. Newspaper reviews are from promotional flyers advertising ATP's lecture series.

2. There was an organized Free Religious Association existing for twenty-five to thirty years, starting in 1867. It was formed as a backlash by the more radical Unitarians who felt disenfranchised by decisions adopted by conservative Unitarians. Half of its members were Unitarian ministers who never withdrew from the denomination. Although no doubt Anita was aware of the movement, her use of the term *Free Thought* seemed to have less to do with that movement and more to do with the New

Thought movement, which drew inspiration from Trancendentalism, Spiritualism, Christian Science, and other metaphysical belief systems. These systems all shared a basic belief in applying religious practices to the life problems of poverty, illness, and unhappiness.

ATP would use the terms *Free Thought* and *New Thought* interchangeably throughout her life, but both seemed to denote her philosophy and her insistence on complete autonomy and freedom to express her personal religion of revelation, inspiration, and intuition. She would later explain, "The New Thought does not require that one be a member of any church, neither does it prohibit [one] from any kind of religious membership." (Printed in a feature story in a St. Louis, Missouri, newspaper, circa 1900.)

She would be quoted in a feature article in the *Philadelphia Sunday Press* as saying, "I am not identified with any religious sect. I go among the members of all religions and am just as much in sympathy with one as with another. Religions after all are not an end; they are gates to the temple of truth, although it is true, that sometimes the gates are so ornate that they are mistaken for the temple itself. I do not care by what gateway you enter so that you will meet me in the Temple of Truth."

3. For a time in the early 1900s, ATP supplemented her lecture income with photography. She illustrated newspaper articles that she wrote and brochures for the Oscawanna Summer Institute and for the Sahler Sanitarium, and created postcards that she sold privately to individuals.

A Public Speaking Career Begins

1. John Dewey, American educator and philosophy professor at Columbia University, said of this man: "It would require less than the fingers of the two hands to enumerate those who, from Plato down, rank with Henry George among the world's social philosophers. . . . No man, no graduate of a higher educational institution, has a right to regard himself as an educated man in social thought unless he has some first hand acquaintance with the theoretical contribution of this great American Thinker."

Spiritual Journey

1. The Spiritualist movement in this country began in 1848 when two young girls, the Fox sisters, in upstate New York—perhaps out of boredom—began to play tricks by rapping on the floor over their parents' heads. (Forty years later, Maggie Fox would reveal that she and her sister Kate were cracking their toe joints to make the sound.) Excitement over these presumed messages from spirits snowballed; psychic phenomena in the form of seances and mediums became the rage on this continent and Europe. By 1868, there were estimated to be eleven million believers in Spiritualism.

    The religious climate of the mid-nineteenth century in the United States, and of New York State in particular, was one of deep disquietude and experimentation. It was a time when self-proclaimed prophets, such as Mary Baker Eddy of the Christian Scientists and Joseph Smith of the Mormons, as well as founders of other new and strongly independent experimental religious communities, found fertile ground in people's hunger for more personal, less dogmatic religious expression. That may help to explain why so many of the brightest minds of the day succumbed to Spiritualism's belief in the blurring of boundaries between life and death, even though the very leaders themselves often boldly proclaimed their fraudulence—seemingly to deaf ears. Many notable intellectuals of the time, author Arthur Conan Doyle among them, were believers. William James, philosopher and writer, was part of the religious and scientific community that was interested enough to try to prove or disprove the validity of Spiritualism. The Shakers embraced Spiritualist beliefs eagerly; a Universalist minister and philanthropist, John Spear, became a spirit medium.

    In 1881 Madame Blavatsky, herself an admitted fraud, founded a church based on Spiritualism—the Theosophical Society, which she saw as a huge joke that she played on the world. It proved never to attract the large following of its parent organization. By the 1920s and 1930s, the religious movement had greatly subsided, but its tentacles—organizations devoted to the study and research of psychic phenomena—continued to flourish. (Brandon, Ruth. *The Spiritualists: The*

175

Passion for the Occult in the Nineteenth and Twentieth Centuries.
New York: Alfred A. Knopf, 1983.)

2. In the mid-nineteenth century, Spiritualist women—trance lecturers—braved and paved the way for other women lecturers, despite the accepted social norms that denied women a public forum, even to an audience of women only and certainly to mixed-gender audiences. They were joined by a growing number of women reformers, a handful of Christian Evangelists, and women authors speaking in literary Lyceum series. (Braude, Ann. *Radical Spirits: Spiritualism and Women's Rights in Nineteenth Century America.* Boston: Beacon Press, 1989.)

   By the time ATP joined the lecture circuit, it was not unusual for women to speak publicly, but her youth and her ability to speak spontaneously drew much attention to her. The Lyceum series and the Chautauquas (based on the Chautauqua Institute in upstate New York, founded in 1874 and still very much alive) were a major source of entertainment and education in small towns and cities across the country. It would seem that popular lecturers were idolized much as movie, stage, and television personalities—as well as sports figures—later came to be. The silver-tongued orator William Jennings Bryan was the biggest attraction on the Chautauqua circuit that began in 1904.

The Vedanta Influence and the Peace Flag

1. According to ATP, the Universal Peace Union was organized in 1866 in Philadelphia by Quakers. Among the far-reaching results produced through its peace efforts was the establishment of the Internation Court of Arbitration.

2. Other recipients of the Peace Flag, besides ATP and Ella Wheeler Wilcox, were the Reverend Alexander F. Irvine of the People's Church in New Haven (Anita served as his assistant there for a while), The Universal Peace Union, The YMCA of New York City, William Randolph Hearst, the New York State Board of Education, and Andrew Carnegie—in recognition of his peace palace at The Hague.

Inspiration for Nature Writing

1. John Burroughs's celery patch is described in detail in *John Burroughs' Slabsides,* written by his granddaughter, Elizabeth Burroughs Kelley. Celery evidently was not a common crop in the Hudson Valley, for it elicited much interest, and, according to John's son, Julian Burroughs, was a "tricky and arduous business."

Public Life as a New Thought Preacher

1. Meadville Theological School, established in 1844 in Pennsylvania, later became Meadville Lombard Theological School, located in Chicago.

Marriage and Family, at Last

1. Elbert Hubbard, writer, lecturer, philosopher, epigrammist, innkeeper, and encourager of arts and crafts, was born in Bloomington, Illinois, in 1856 and died in the sinking of the S.S. *Lusitania* by a German U-boat in 1915. His most famous work, *A Message to Garcia,* sold an estimated four million copies and was on the bestseller list for many years. During Hubbard's lifetime, he successfully pursued his dream of fashioning an American counterpart to William Morris's English crafts complex. The Roycroft complex in East Aurora, New York, left an indelible stamp on the American Arts and Crafts movement. Although the original institution was closed during the depression of the 1930s, today the fourteen buildings have been designated a national historic landmark. One can visit the museum run by the Aurora Historical Society (June through October, Wednesdays, Saturdays, and Sundays, 2–4 P.M. or by appointment, 716/652-4735), stay at the Roycroft Inn—once the print shop—or tour many of the artisans' shops. Tours may be arranged by calling 716/655-0571.

Finally—Ordination to Unitarian Ministry

1. W. C. Gannett had been a long-time supporter of women's rights and woman's place in the ministry. As a close friend of

Jenkin Lloyd Jones, who was the Unitarian Western Conference secretary and, according to Cynthia Grant Tucker in *Prophetic Sisterhood,* "was unsurpassed in his feminist zeal and stamina. . . . worked for the cause for so many years that by the time he was in his seventies, he was billing himself as 'America's aboriginal suffragist.'" Tucker refers to Jones and Gannett as "the rare brother feminists."

First Ministries: Rowe Camp and Barnard Memorial

1. When Sophia Lyons Fahs—tireless religious education worker for the Unitarian denomination for nearly thirty years—gave her own ordination sermon in 1959, she noted that, in the AUA Year Book listing of ministers, there were only 6 women out of a total of 539—and of these few, all but one were retired.

2. This entry is a total puzzlement, as Anita's autobiography positively teems with dozens of friends' names—with many of whom she stayed for various lengths of time.

Readings

1
The Advance of the People

Advance, ye sons of freedom! Sons of light!
  Your enemies are not your fellowmen.
Against the power of Ignorance ye fight.
And ye must slay him o'er and o'er again.

On every hand his banner is unfurled.
Where'er ye turn, his influence is known.
His dread oppression circles round the world—
And ye may vanquish him with truth alone.

This giant is the foe that we must face.
United, we are strong to overcome,
And blot from our fair land the faintest trace
Of his oppression. Not by sword and drum

Or outward show shall we the conquerors be
  But, pressing forward in the cause of right
And justice, bound by truth and loyalty,
To spread the advent of the Age of Light.
We recognize no party, creed or power.
We fight against the common foe of all.
United, in one grand triumphant hour,
Victorious, we shall see oppression's fall.

Advance, then, soldiers in the cause of right!
  Yield not an inch until your cause be won!
The golden era dawns upon your sight,
Oh, spirit of our Prophet, lead thou on!

Anita Trueman, 1897

2
The Fall of Man
(Excerpt)

. . . And still another voice its message brings.
Borne on the evening breeze, it whispers low,
And I am startled, for the mystic sound
Comes not from earth or sky, from woods or stream,
But from within my soul, in accents low
it speaks; "Be still and know that I am God."
"Speak, Lord! Thy servant heareth" I reply.
Then, as I listen, accents rich and sweet
Fill all the ancient grove with melody.
Know then, O Man, that through the ages past,
Before the sun on high his circuit ran,
Even before the Universe had form,
Intelligence could speak the words, "I AM!"
Intelligence was all, and by His word
All things created were, the earth, the sea,
The firmament, and all that in them is.
And over all the law of harmony
Held potent sway; and when the work was done,
Then to complete the work, and crown it all,
He built a glorious temple, fair and good,
Where he might dwell, and from it issue forth
His will and blessing to His universe.
"Tis good!" the monarch said, when all was done,
And in his temple fair his home was made.
But, as he gazed in rapture o'er the scene,
He fell asleep, and dreamed a direful dream.
Out from the beauteous earth, it seemed, there came
A serpent, Ignorance, whose awful sway
Held e'en the God within its dreadful power.
Into the lovely fane the serpent crept,
Bringing to that fair palace Death's decay.
And when Intelligence looked forth again
The powers which once he wielded seemed to be
All-powerful to destroy and rule their king.

And still he slept. But once, upon his sleep
The Light of Consciousness its radiance beamed.
But Ignorance still held him in its power,
So to that Light he bowed but did not grasp
Its flame, and wield his own unbounded power.
But still He followed it.
                    "Know Thou, O Man,
That heareth this, it is Thy history.
Intelligence embodied, I am come,
The Light of Consciousness, to lead thee home,
To teach thee of thy nature. Know Thyself!"
Thou art the King of all this universe.
It is thy thought, created by thy power.
Wake, ye who slumber, to the glorious day!
While ye have slept, the law of harmony
Hath kept its power, and all that ye have seen
Of discord, death, subjection, and decay,
Are but the phantoms of your ignorance.
Oh, dream no longer, Man! Arise and claim
The power that waiteth for thy guiding hand.
Awake! Thou hast not yet the beauties seen
Of thy fair universe. Thy limbs are stiff
With sleeping through the ages. Let the life
Of thy true being course along thy veins,
And make the temple glorious as before.
Soar through the wide and limitless expanse
Of thy creation. See thy thought expressed
in harmony divine. Forget thy dream
And know of nothing but the truth and love
That fill thy universe. Come! Claim thy bride
And take her home. Her name is Harmony.
Be fruitful, Man, and multiply thy kind.
Fill all the earth with Truth and Liberty,
Confidence, Love, these shall thy children be.
Perfection is thy law, Infinity
Thy nature, and thy goal, Eternity.

                                        Anita Trueman, 1897

3
Knowledge and Faith

Every human being lays hold upon life, as it were, by two hands, knowledge and faith. Knowledge is the firm right hand which directly governs our actions. Faith assists knowledge to bring new objects within its grasp, and to hold them till they have been fully examined. It sounds the rich bass chords which accompany and support the melody of our lives. It holds the negative pole of the circuit which connects us with the battery of spiritual force that sustains our individual existence.

Some few persons are spiritually left-handed, neglecting knowledge, and accepting faith as their guide in life. They are dreamy and unsatisfactory folks, on the whole; while those who emphasize knowledge and ignore faith are limited in their activities and harsh in their judgments. The well-balanced life is spiritually ambidextrous, and has the wide reach and firm hold which only knowledge and faith working together can bring.

We are in the habit of thinking that we derive our knowledge and our faith from the established and institutionalized Science and Religion of the world about us. But in reality the reverse is true. Knowledge and faith are elements of our human constitution, as surely as hands and feet, nerves and organs of sense. We must use and develop them, in order to expand our mental horizon, as we have learned to use the telescope and the telephone to extend the range of our senses. The evolution of knowledge and faith produces, by natural but complex processes, that vast world of consciousness whose kingdoms are known as Science, Philosophy, and Religion.

The human mind, through ages of thought, has built up the great structure of classified knowledge called Science; it has crystalized its questioning and theories in regard to the Nature of things into various schools of Philosophy; and it has justified its faith in many forms of Religion. But these have all grown out of men and must grow out of them still. Our heritage from the past is useless to us, unless we prove and employ it ourselves, and improve it as we pass it on.

We have each, as our natural endowment, the instinct of knowledge and the impulse of faith. Through observation and comparison we furnish ourselves with the elementary knowledge which is our working capital in the business of life; but at the same time we respond to the lure of the unknown, we delight in the pursuit of mystery, we apprehend a Reality greater than we can define, we accept the authority of others in matters beyond our experience. In all this, the impulse of faith is leading us beyond the limitations of our present knowledge, but the desire to know follows faith into this realm, and finds there many jewels to add to its treasures of truth. Information concerning facts beyond the range of our senses, inventions which put us in command of greater power, ideals which enhance all the values of our lives, come to us through the channel of Faith. But knowledge must appropriate them to suitable service in our lives.

We must understand that the world's Science, Philosophy, and Religion are meaningless to us, unless we are ourselves scientific, philosophical, and religious in our way of thinking. We must accept on faith most of the teachings of modern Science, they are so far beyond popular comprehension, and require such elaborate methods of demonstration. A whole world of knowledge, thoroughly tested and classified, is necessary to place at our service the telephone which is so essential a part of domestic as well as business economy in these days. But very few of us possess even a fragment of this knowledge, and the same is true of almost every article we use. We accept all this on faith, but how much more it would mean to us, if we kept the instinct of knowledge alert! We might be scientific, and philosophical, and even religious in relation to the telephone, as well as practical, if we chose, and this would make us worth far more to others, more precious to ourselves.

Whenever we try to classify any item of knowledge in its orderly relation to any other knowledge we may possess or be able to obtain, we are scientific; when we are curious as to the cause of any phenomenon, we are philosophical, and when we seek the universal beyond the particular, and respond to its mystery and majesty, we are religious. These attitudes of mind are characteristic of the growing life in us, and as we cultivate them we reach beyond all limitations. These are the keys of power, but we must use them for ourselves. To merely accept the work of others will not do. We may enjoy the fruits of their labors, but only as slaves may we enjoy the luxury of their masters. Let us be freemen in the world of thought, and true comrades of those great souls who are the builders of human history.

Anita Trueman Pickett, 1911
Unity Church, Boise, Idaho

4
Take Thy Light

Take up thy light and let it gleam
Upon the upward winding way
Where, silently, as in a dream,
Our band of friends goes up to pray

Bring in thy light, and let its ray
Be added to the growing light
Which makes the chapel, old and gray,
A beacon on its rocky height

Lift up thy light, a gift of love,
And hang it on the sacred cross,
A symbol of that light above
Which sanctifies all pain and loss

Take forth thy light, nor let its flame
Be quenched as carried candles are,
But let thy life in love proclaim
The message of our Island Star

Words: Anita Trueman Pickett
Tune: Missionary Chant
Written at Star Island, 1927, and sung in the chapel

5
Grinding the Georgean Axe

To an old Single Taxer, one who worked with Henry George in that last campaign when he gave his life for the cause of individual liberty and social justice which is the gospel embodied in *Progress and Poverty,* this phrase was a challenge, and I wanted to talk back. But reflecting that in these days the foreground of thought is cluttered with Marxianism and its one-time enemy, Fascism, and that the classroom economics which young men absorb relegates the simple and comprehensive truth of "Georgeanism" to a neglected pigeonhole, I smothered the impulse.

Lately, however, it seems that the Communists have entered my name on their mailing lists, for I am getting a great variety of propaganda material from them, . . . So before the Dies Committee enrolls me on its blacklist, I would like to declare to those who may be concerned that after sympathetically considering Communism, Socialism, and Fascism, I am still a Single Taxer. I believe that nothing is more important for Americans at this time than to reconsider the gospel taught by that "man sent of God, whose name was Henry George," to quote Edward McGlynn's tribute at George's funeral, to which the huge crowd assembled in New York's Grand Central Palace responded with a cheer!

That cheer still rings in my heart, after forty-three years of the public service to which I dedicated my life as I looked on our lost leader's dead face that day. Here was an American patriot as brave as any who ever went down to death on a battlefield, a philosopher and economist whose legacy to his native land is a gift which we should now take from the vault of our treasure house, and use before it is too late. It can cure our domestic disorder and defend us from the infection of anti-American virus, which would destroy all individual liberty, and make our country a battlefield of class warfare.

Here is a doctrine which had its birth on American soil, and embodies that faith in the individual citizen which is the soul of American democracy. It proclaims that every individual should be secure in the possession and use of all that he can earn or produce. At the same time, the community is entitled to those values which its existence creates, and if these were turned over to its administrative offices, there would be no need for any other form of taxation. Yet all public needs could be served generously, and a surplus for constructive improvements would be constantly accumulating.

Land has no value until people want it, or what it contains, and are willing to pay for the privilege of using it. What they are willing to pay is its rental value, and should be collected by the community. A city lot which was once bought for a glass bead is now worth thousands of dollars. If the city had been taking its growing rental value as revenue all these years, it would have been able to carry on all its business without levying taxes on industry, improvements, income, or consumption. But it would have few millionaires.

A cliff in Canada which recently was worthless wilderness has now become more precious than a pile of diamonds, because so many sufferers need the radium it contains. The Curies gave their great discovery to the world without price. The discoverers of this cliff are entitled to some bonus for the labors of exploration, and the scientists and engineers and other workers who mine and refine the ore are entitled to generous compensation. But that cliff belongs to Canada, and no monopoly should be allowed to build private fortunes out of it.

The Georgean method of raising public revenue would make it impossible for speculators to gamble with the fruits of other people's labor, or for monopolists to get from the possession of natural resources the unearned profits which they now re-invest in more monopolies. For an influential minority in this country such power to fleece the populace is a privilege which they fiercely defend, misnaming it "business enterprise."

On the other hand, the left-wingers admit that the Single Tax "is all right as far as it goes." But they are not satisfied to let the community exercise its rights of eminent domain, and take for its common fund the rental value of all land within its territory, leaving individuals free in the use of that land, and in the possession of all they can produce from it. They want to "socialize" the labor and buildings and machinery too, and to regulate consumption and distribution in the arbitrary way which makes so much difficulty in the Soviet Republics.

It is true that modern industry is organized on a huge scale, and scientific methods require the cooperation of many specialists, so that the product of labor and skill is collective in many occupations.

Certainly the immense and complicated machines used in modern industry and agriculture cannot be produced or owned individually. But there is nothing in personal liberty to prevent voluntary organization in cooperative enterprises. The economy and efficiency achieved would be for the general good, however, benefitting alike the producers, consumers, and the state; for such corporations, under the Georgean system, would pay their full share of taxation in the rental value of such land (including natural resources) as would necessarily form the basis of all their activities, instead of putting their surplus into the pockets of idle stockholders.

Much has been said in these recent months about the multitudes of persons who are on government payrolls. People who all their lives have lived on the labor of others, refer to those who have been compelled to work for alphabetical agencies during this depression, as "eating out of the public trough." The owner of a fine private estate, whose income from investments has been somewhat reduced, will use this as an excuse to discharge two gardeners, and then complain about the government hiring unemployed boys to clean up our neglected forest, build roads and post offices, and in many other ways improve and protect our public domain. The inference is that we as a nation cannot afford to do these things. Certainly they need to be done, and we could richly afford to do them, if we had a sensible, equitable system of taxation.

There are scores of other ways in which the use of this simple, fundamental remedy would act to cure our domestic ills and to protect us from foreign dangers, mental, economic, or military. A study of the experiments tried in other lands, shows that as far as they are successful, they have employed this principle. Their troubles begin with their suppression of individual liberty and initiative. They are obliged to correct this error by bloody purges, and to rule by the use of terror. We in America still believe in the individual, and his inalienable right to life, liberty, and the pursuit of happiness. We reject the Marxian hypothesis that the individual is the natural foe of society, and must be used as so much man-power, under the dictatorship of the Proletariat, or any other form of dictatorship.

But we have given away our timber lands, our mining lands, much of our water-power lands, and while our country is still very sparsely populated, we seem to have reached our frontiers, and our population is not increasing fast enough to sustain the kind of "prosperity" to which we were accustomed in our youth, with its picturesque overnight fortunes. We must realistically face the fact that we are grown up, consider the vast resources which we have inherited in our territory, and the great gifts of genius which are flowering in technology and in art, the broad spread of education and culture among our people, the skills of craftsmen and mechanics, and plan to dissolve the congestion which prevents the circulation of all this real wealth among its creators.

We can justify our possession of this heritage only if we can prove to the rest of the world that we can administer it for the general welfare. "The Earth is the Lord's, and the fullness thereof, the World and they that dwell therein." But let us remember that "the Earth hath He given to the children of men."

Anita Trueman Pickett, circa 1940

Chronology

1881	Annie Trueman is born in Cleveland, Ohio
1881	Moves to Birmingham, England
1891	Returns to live in USA, Brooklyn, New York
1896	Is valedictorian of grade school
1897	Gives first lecture at Brooklyn College of Music and Metaphysics
1897	Is involved in the Henry George campaign
1897	Chooses name "Anita"
1897	Publishes *Philo-Sophia*
1898	Moves to New Haven
1898	Begins friendship with Ella Wheeler Wilcox
1898–99	Publishes first poems
1898	Publishes first essays
1899	Begins friendship with Edwin Markham
1900	Moves to Boston, attends Emerson College of Oratory
1900	Publishes second edition of *Philo-Sophia*
1900	Gives first lecture tour
1900	Begins friendship with Swami Abhedananda
1901	Begins involvement with Peace Flag
1901	Makes first visit to Roycroft

1901	Gives first lectures at a Unitarian church
1902	Makes first visit to Sahler Sanitarium, Kingston, New York
1903	Publishes book *Anton's Angels*
1903	Begins friendship with John Burroughs
1905	Father buys family farm in Kingston, New York
1905	Works as assistant editor and secretary to Dr. Patterson on New Thought magazine, *Mind*
1906	Lives at Vedanta House, New York City
1907	Lectures at Meadville Theological Seminary in exchange for tuition
1907	Meets Harold Pickett at Meadville
1908	Marries Harold Pickett
1909	Gives birth to first child, Estelle
1909	Assists Harold at Sandwich, Massachusetts Unitarian Church
1910	Assists Harold at Boise, Idaho church and serves as pastor of the junior congregation
1911	Gives birth to second child, Trueman
1912–21	Preaches fifty-four times at fifteen Unitarian churches
1913	Gives birth to third child, Laurel
1920	Serves as supply minister at Stoneham, Massachusetts
1921	Is ordained as Unitarian minister, Woburn, Massachusetts
1921–26	Serves first single ministry as summer minister at Rowe, Massachusetts
1921–22	Serves as superintendent of Barnard Memorial Church in Boston, Massachusetts
1923	Is instrumental in starting Rowe Camp

1923–25	Is elected Clerk of the Unitarian Sunday School Society and the Department of Religious Education of the AUA.
1923–26	Serves joint ministry with husband at Peabody, Massachusetts
1926–28	Serves joint ministry with husband at Medfield, Massachusetts
1927–28	Serves joint ministry with husband at Walpole, Massachusetts
1930–35	Serves single ministry at Barnstable, Massachusetts
1930–40	Preaches often at husband's church, Nantucket, Massachusetts
1937–42	Serves single ministry at Bedford, Massachusetts
1943–47	Serves joint ministry with husband at Dighton, Massachusetts
1945–47	Serves joint ministry with husband at Eastondale, Massachusetts
1950	Harold dies
1950–52	Serves single ministry at Ware, Massachusetts
1951	Publishes book *How Luke Discovered Christmas*
1952	Retires from ministry at Ware, Massachusetts, writes unpublished autobiography and supplies Unitarian Universalist pulpits all over the country
1960	Dies in Kingston, New York

Bibliography

Brandon, Ruth. *The Spiritualists: The Passion for the Occult in the Nineteenth and Twentieth Centuries.* New York: Alfred A. Knopf, 1983.

Braude, Ann. *Radical Spirits: Spiritualism and Women's Rights in Nineteenth-Century America.* Boston: Beacon Press, 1989.

Cazden, Elizabeth. *Antoinette Brown Blackwell: A Biography.* Old Westbury, NY: Feminist Press, 1983.

George, Henry. *Progress and Poverty.* 50th anniversary edition. New York: Robert Schalkenbach Foundation, 1942.

Heilbrun, Carolyn. *Writing a Woman's Life.* New York: Ballantine Books, 1988.

Kelley, Elizabeth Burroughs. *John Burroughs: Naturalist.* West Park, NY: Riverby Books, 1986.

Kelley, Elizabeth Burroughs. *John Burroughs' Slabsides.* Rhinebeck, NY: The Moran Printing Company, 1974.

Kelley, Elizabeth Burroughs. *John Burroughs' Slabsides.* West Park, NY: Riverby Books, 1987.

Miller, Russell E. *The Larger Hope.* Boston: Unitarian Universalist Association, 1979.

Peden, W. Creighton. "Francis Ellingwood Abbot: Prophet of Free Religion." *Proceedings of the Unitarian Universalist Historical Society,* Vol. XXII, Part 1. Cambridge, MA: 1992.

Pickett, Anita Trueman. *How Luke Discovered Christmas.* Boston: The Beacon Press, 1951.

Reuther, Rosemary Radford, and Rosemary Skinner Keller, eds. *Women and Religion in America,* Vol. 3—1900–1968. Windsor, CA: National Women's History Project, 1986.

Trine, Ralph Waldo. *In Tune with the Infinite.* Indianapolis, IN: Bobbs-Merrill, 1908.

Tucker, Cynthia Grant. *Prophetic Sisterhood: Liberal Women Ministers of the Frontier 1880–1930.* Boston: Beacon Press, 1990.

Wilbur, Earl Morse. *A History of Unitarianism.* Boston: Beacon Press, 1978.

Photographs, sermon notes, newspaper articles, at Andover–Newton Library archives of the Harvard Divinity School, Cambridge, Massachusetts.

Photographs, letters, diaries—at Rowe Camp and Conference Center, Rowe, Massachusetts.

Photographs, diaries, unpublished autobiography ("Grandmanita's Youth"), newspaper clippings—at homes of Anita Trueman Pickett's family members.